T0063990

GOOD
TO THE LAST OUT

TO THE LAST OUT

The Encyclopedia of the Last Out of the World Series

THEO TATE

authorHOUSE®

AuthorHouse™ LLC
1663 Liberty Drive
Bloomington, IN 47403
www.authorhouse.com
Phone: 1-800-839-8640

© 2014 Theo Tate. All rights reserved.

No part of this book may be reproduced, stored in
a retrieval system, or transmitted by any means
without the written permission of the author.

Published by AuthorHouse 06/12/2014

ISBN: 978-1-4969-1715-7 (sc)
ISBN: 978-1-4969-1714-0 (e)

Library of Congress Control Number: 2014910082

Any people depicted in stock imagery provided by Thinkstock are models,
and such images are being used for illustrative purposes only.
Certain stock imagery © Thinkstock.

This book is printed on acid-free paper.

Because of the dynamic nature of the Internet, any web addresses or
links contained in this book may have changed since publication and
may no longer be valid. The views expressed in this work are solely those
of the author and do not necessarily reflect the views of the publisher,
and the publisher hereby disclaims any responsibility for them.

CONTENTS

PREFACE

After 45 years, Major League Baseball got a Triple Crown winner in 2012.

That's a long time to wait for another Triple Crown winner.

Carl Yastremski was the last Triple Crown winner in 1967. Back then, baseball didn't have to wait 45 years to get a Triple Crown winner. Frank Robinson won it the year before while playing for the Orioles. Mickey Mantle won it 1956. Ted Williams won it twice in 1942 and 1947. Jimmie Foxx, Chuck Klein, Lou Gehrig and Ducky Medwick also won Triple Crowns in the 1930s. Rogers Hornsby won it in 1922 and 1925.

So there were no Triple Crown winners in the 1970s, 1980s, 1990s or 2000s. Baseball had to go through six commissioners to finally celebrate a Triple Crown. There were expansion, more expansion, free agency, lockout and a season-ending strike happening during those 45 years.

Before 1967, the Triple Crown wasn't hard to accomplish. Now, the Triple Crown has become more difficult to accomplish. But getting the Triple Crown wasn't difficult for Miguel Cabrera. He hit 44 home runs, drove in 139 runs and batted .330 to end a 45-year drought. Plus, Cabrera is the third living Triple Crown winner (the others are Yastremski and Robinson).

Cabrera's team was really good as well. The Tigers won the American League Central and went on to sweep the

Yankees in the American League Championship Series to go to the World Series.

So far in 2012, everything was cruising for Cabrera. He was a Triple Crown winner and was going to the World Series.

On October 28, Cabrera was about to make history. But it was a feat that he didn't have in mind. Of all of the home runs, RBIs and hits he put together in 2012, none of it would erase on what happened to him in the bottom of the 10th in Game 4 of the 2012 World Series against the San Francisco Giants at Comerica Park.

Cabrera was facing Sergio Romo with two outs and his Tigers were trailing 4-3. With the Tigers down 3 games to 0, all of Detroit wanted Cabrera to get a home run or get a hit to continue the Tigers' season. But what Tiger fans saw was Cabrera becoming the first Triple Crown winner to be the final out of the World Series.

Cabrera struck out looking. Romo, catcher Buster Posey and all of the Giants celebrated near the pitching mound. It was San Francisco's second title in three years, but getting it wasn't easy. The Giants came back from a 2 games to 0 deficit to beat Cincinnati in the National League Division Series, then came back from 3-1 down to beat the 2011 champion St. Louis Cardinals.

On that October 28 night in Detroit, Romo helped the Giants end the baseball season by striking out a giant killer at the plate.

That is why baseball is so good to the final out. When any player gets the final out, a bunch of grown men start acting like kids and celebrate until the break of dawn. That's what makes baseball so great.

Ending the baseball season with a strikeout is now becoming a trend in the World Series. In the last eight World Series, six of them ended with a strikeout. When he was asked by FOX Sports reporter Ken Rosenthal about how does it feel to get the final out, Romo replied, "I'm blessed."

That night, my sister Darlene, who lives in the Atlanta, Georgia area, was visiting me at my home in O'Fallon, Illinois and watching TV. I had to interrupt Darlene's TV watching so I can record the final out on my VCR. I always like to record the final out of the World Series. When I saw that strikeout on TV, I told my sister that I'm going to write a book – a book chronicling of the final out of the World Series and the inside stories of the final out of the World Series in a "position-by-position" format.

I looked forward to watching the World Series since 1982. The best part of watching the World Series is the final out. It's always something everyone dreams about for over 100 years. Even I dreamed about making the final out the World Series when I had dreams of becoming a baseball player. One day, you're playing in T-ball, the next day, you make the final out of the World Series.

I finally went to my first World Series game on October 27, 2013, when the Cardinals played the Red Sox in game four of the Fall Classic at Busch Stadium. When I decided to get tickets for this game, I thought I would see the final out of the World Series in that game because after all, the Fall Classic ended in a sweep the year before. So I thought either the Red Sox or Cardinals would finish in a sweep. Those plans were put on hold after the two teams split their first two games at Boston, meaning that I wasn't going to see the final out of the World Series in game four. But I did see Kolten Wong getting picked off at first to end the game and tie the Series at two games apiece. It's the first time a World Series game was ended with a runner getting picked off. But the World Series was *never* ended with a runner being picked off. What it would have been like had Wong was the final out of the World Series?

The final out can be recorded in many different ways. It can be a strikeout, groundout, a double play, a triple play, a force out, a pop up to the outfield, a pop up to the infield, a pop up to the infield or runner's interference.

Even the final out can be recorded with a runner trying to steal a base. Just ask the Yankees' Babe Ruth. But who threw him out?

Even the final out can be recorded by snatching a line drive from a hitter, stealing his dreams of helping his team win the World Series. Just ask the Yankees' Bobby Richardson. But who hit the line drive?

Even players cringe of being the final out of World Series. What former famous baseball broadcaster was the final out of the 1968 Fall Classic?

I remember watching Bruce Sutter striking out Gorman Thomas for the final out of the 1982 World Series on a black and white TV set in the kitchen of my house in St. Louis when I was 7 years old. That was the night that my love of baseball blossomed. Several months before, I went to my first baseball game as the Cardinals were playing the Phillies at Busch Stadium.

When he struck out Gorman Thomas for the final out, Bruce Sutter and Darrell Porter hugged each other. It was a highlight that would be played over and over and over again, even the time when Sutter was inducted into the Baseball Hall of Fame. During the summer of 1983, Darlene and I imitated Sutter and Porter while we were in the backyard of our house. I was the catcher and Darlene was the pitcher. Darlene, who is now a football fan, threw a pitch to me and we pretended that Milwaukee slugger Gorman Thomas was at the plate. After Darlene threw a pitch to me, we ran into each other and hugged just like Sutter and Porter did. It was the final out in the '82 World Series that caught my attention for baseball. I became a baseball fan because not only the Cardinals won the World Series, but it was because of that final out. It was amazing to see more than 50,000 folks run onto the field to celebrate. I never thought baseball was that exciting.

At the end of the 2013 season, a total of 96 players made the final out of the World Series. This year, there are over 700 grown men playing major league baseball. By the time playoffs start in October, that number will be sliced to 250. When the World Series arrives, that number will be cut to 50. Out of those 50, twenty five of them will celebrate as world champs.

Out of those 25, one of them will be the 97th player to make the final out of the World Series (unless the World Series ends in a walk-off).

There were 11 World Series that were decided on either a hit, a wild pitch or a sacrifice fly. Sorry, Luis Gonzalez, Edgar Renteria, Joe Carter, Gene Larkin, Bill Mazeroski, Billy Martin, Goose Goslin and Earl McNeely. This book is not about you guys. This book is paying homage to the players who made the final out in one of the greatest sporting events ever.

This book will show that baseball can be good to the last out.

CHAPTER ONE: PITCHER

By striking out Miguel Cabrera in the 2012 World Series, Sergio Romo is in good company. He's one of 19 pitchers who ended the World Series with a strikeout. In the 110-year history of the World Series, a total of 25 pitchers recorded the final out of the Fall Classic, more than any other position.

Koji Uehara became pitcher No. 25 on October 30, 2013. That night, the Red Sox won their eighth title by beating St. Louis in six games, but they did something they hadn't done since 1918 – clinch a World Series championship at home.

Uehara helped the Sox accomplish that feat by striking out the Cardinals' Matt Carpenter with no runners on and two outs at Fenway Park. The 38-year-old Uehara retired the side in the ninth to help the Red Sox record a 6-1 victory. He also became the first Japanese player to get the final out of the World Series.

Photo by Keith Allison; http://commons. wikimedia.org/wiki/File:Koji_ Uehara_2_on_June_15,_2013.jpg

Uehara is one of seven Japanese players who won a World Series title. His Red Sox teammate, Junichi Tazawa, is also in that group.

Uehara was born on April 3, 1975 in Neyagawa, Osaka, Japan. Before joining the major leagues in 2009, Uehara played with the Yomiuri Giants for nine years from 1999 to 2008. In his rookie season with Yomiuri, Uehara won 15 straight games that broke the all-time rookie record.

In 2006, he helped Team Japan win the gold medal at the World Baseball Classic in San Diego. Two years before, Uehara helped Team Japan finish with a bronze medal in the 2004 Olympic Games at Athens, Greece.

After three seasons with Baltimore and two with Texas, Uehara joined the Red Sox in 2013 and became pretty valuable, finishing with a career-best 21 saves, winning an American League Championship Series Most Valuable Player award and helping Boston become the first team since the 1991 Minnesota Twins to win a World Series after finishing last the previous year.

The Red Sox won 97 games, tying the Cardinals for the best record in baseball. They dedicated their season to the victims of the Boston Marathon bombing, where two explosions killed three people at the race on April 15. Boston advanced to the World Series by beating Tampa Bay in four games in the ALDS and Detroit in six games in the ALCS.

Uehara finished with seven saves in the 2013 postseason, tying a record mark set by four other pitchers. He also got the last out in both the ALDS and the ALCS. Uehara struck out Tampa Bay's Evan Longoria in the fourth game of the ALDS in Tropicana Field and Detroit's Jose Iglesias in the sixth game of the ALCS at Fenway Park.

By striking out Carpenter, the 38-year-old Uehara helped the Red Sox win their third World Series in 10 seasons. Before 2004, Boston was on an 86-year World Series championship drought.

***

The World Series celebrated its 110th anniversary in 2013. Coincidentally, Boston won the first World Series and a pitcher got the final out. That pitcher was Bill Dinneen.

Dinneen was born in Syracuse, New York in 1876, the same year the National League was founded. The National League represented the top level of organized baseball in the United States. From 1871 to 1875, the National League was known as the National Association of Professional Baseball Players.

In the National League, all championships are awarded to the team with the best record at the end of the season and no postseason series was played. From 1884-1890, the National League and the American Association, which was formed in 1882, played each other in a series of games at the end of the season to determine an overall champion, and the series was promoted and referred to as the The Championship of the United States, World's Championship Series or World's Series for short.

After the American Association folded in 1891, the National League was again the only major league. In 1892, the league championship was awarded by a playoff between half-season champions. The next year, a champion was awarded to the first-place club in the standings. Then for four years, the league champions played the runners-up in the postseason championship series called the Temple Cup, then the Chronicle-Telegraph Cup in 1900.

The American League was formed as a second major league in 1901, but no championship series was played until 1903, when the Boston Americans faced the Pittsburgh Pirates in the first World Series.

The Boston Americans were formed in 1901 as one of the American League's eight charter franchises. They finished second to the Chicago White Sox with a 79-57 record. That same year, Dinneen played with the Boston Beaneaters, who finished 69-69 in the National League. He played two years with the Beaneaters, who later became the Boston, then Milwaukee, now Atlanta Braves. He also played with the Washington Senators in the National League in 1898 and 1899.

In 1902, Dinneen joined the Boston Americans and finished with a 21-21 record on the mound, but his 21 losses led the American League.

The next year, Dinneen not only finished with a winning record (21-13) and a league-best two saves, but he also helped the Americans win the first modern World Series in come-from-behind fashion.

The Americans, who won 91 games to capture the American League pennant, came back from a 3 games to 1 deficit to beat the National League champion Pittsburgh Pirates in eight games in the best of nine World Series.

The 27-year-old Dinneen clinched the Americans' championship by striking out future Hall of Famer Honus Wagner with two outs in the top of the ninth in game eight at Huntington Avenue Baseball Grounds in Boston (This was way before the days of Fenway Park).

Not only he got the final out of the 1903 season, Dinneen also set a World Series record for strikeouts with 11, breaking the old record of 10 set by Pittsburgh's Deacon Phillippe in Game 7. Dinneen struck out seven and pitched a complete-game victory in Game 8, with Boston winning 3-0 and the series 5 games to 3. Dinneen would never play in another World Series game.

The next year, Dinneen could have played in another World Series. He helped the Americans win another American League pennant, but the National League champion New York Giants declined to participate in the World Series, calling the American League "a junior league." So there was no World Series in 1904. That year, Dinneen turned in another strong season on the mound, winning a career-high 23 games.

But after going 20-38 in the next three years at Boston, Dinneen was sent to the St. Louis Browns, where he would spend three seasons before retiring in 1909. By that time, the Americans had changed their name to the Red Sox.

***

After Dinneen, baseball had to wait another 22 years to see the World Series end with a strikeout.

Under rainy conditions at Forbes Field in Pittsburgh in game seven of the 1925 World Series, the Pirates' Red Oldham got the Washington Senators' Goose Goslin on a called third strike to give the Bucs their second world championship.

The 32-year-old Oldham pitched a 1-2-3 ninth inning and all three batters he faced were later inducted into the Hall of Fame. Goslin struck out Sam Rice looking, got Bucky Harris on a groundout to second base and struck out Goslin looking.

Pittsburgh beat Washington 9-7 to win the Series 4 games to 3 and prevented the Senators from winning their second straight crown. It's also the first time the Pirates won a world title in front of their home fans. Forbes Field was built in 1909, the same year the Bucs won their first title, but they clinched it on the road.

John Cyrus Oldham was born on July 15, 1893 in Zion, Maryland, which is an unincorporated community in Cecil County, which is located in the northeast part of the state.

Oldham played in seven non-consecutive seasons in the majors. He started his career in 1914 with the Tigers. After going 3-0 in 1915, Oldham was released by the Tigers and was sent to the San Francisco Seals of the Pacific Coast League.

Oldham returned to the Tigers in 1920 and played for three more seasons. He won a career-high 11 games in 1921.

After a two-year hiatus, Oldham was back in the majors, this time with the Pirates. He helped the Bucs win 95 games and their third National League pennant. Oldham pitched in 11 games and was 3-2 with a 3.91 ERA.

Oldham appeared in the 1925 World Series for the first time when he came in relief for Ray Kremer in the top of the ninth. He played in the World Series for the first and only time in his pro baseball career.

After having a career-high 5.62 earned run average in 1926, Oldham retired. He died on January 28, 1961 at age 67 at Costa Mesa, California.

***

New York Giants pitcher Dolf Luque picked up another World Series championship on October 7, 1933.

By striking out the Washington Senators' Joe Kuhel in the bottom of the 10th inning in game five of the World Series, Luque won his third World Series title. He also played on World Series championship teams with the Braves (1914) and Reds (1919).

The Giants beat Washington 4-3 to win the Series four games to one and capture their fourth World Series title. It was the last time the Senators played in the World Series.

Luque became the first of 10 players from outside the United States to get the final out of the World Series. The others are Hector Lopez (1961), Jackie Hernandez (1971), Bert Campaneris (1973), Cesar Geronimo (1975), Omar Moreno (1979), Bernie Williams (2000), Juan Uribe (2005), Robinson Cano (2009) and Koji Uehara (2013).

Luque is nicknamed the Pride of Havana because he was born and raised in Havana, Cuba on Aug. 4, 1890. Founded by the Spanish in the 16th century, Havana is a big tourist attraction, drawing over a million visitors annually. Havana is also Cuba's capital and has over two million people living there.

Luque played winter baseball in the Cuban League for 33 years. He was elected to the Cuban Baseball Hall of Fame in 1957.

Luque began his major league career in 1914 with the Braves, who stunned the Philadelphia A's in the World Series that year. Luque was traded to the Reds in 1918 and helped them win it all in 1919.

Luque played with the Reds for 12 seasons before heading to Brooklyn in 1932 to play for the Robins (now Dodgers). Then, Luque joined the Giants in 1932.

In 1933, Luque helped the Giants win their first world title in 11 years with his solid relief pitching. He led the National League with eight wins in relief, and picked up four saves.

Luque picked up the win in game five of the 1933 World Series, his only win in postseason play. He came in relief for Hal Schumacher with two outs in the bottom of the sixth with the game tied at three. With the Senators having runners on first and third, Luque got Luke Sewell to ground out to second.

The Giants took a 4-3 lead on a solo home run by Mel Ott in the top of the 10th.

Luque got the first two outs of the bottom of the 10th before giving up a single to Joe Cronin and a walk to Fred Schulte. The Senators' rally – and the 1933 season -- ended after Luque struck out Kuhel.

Luque gave up no runs on two hits, struck out five and walked two in four and one-third innings in relief. It was Luque's only appearance in the Series. At age 43, Luque is the oldest player to get the final out of the World Series.

Luque played two more seasons with the Giants before retiring as a player with 194 wins, 1,130 strikeouts and 28 saves. He was the Giants' pitching coach from 1936-1937 and 1942-1945. Luque died on July 3, 1957 at age 66 in Havana.

***

With 11 World Series championships, the St. Louis Cardinals won more titles than any other National League team. The Cardinals ended the World Series on a strikeout in four of those.

Ted Wilks was the first of four St. Louis Cardinal pitchers to end a World Series with a strikeout in 1944. In game six of the Fall Classic against the St. Louis Browns at Sportsman's Park, Wilks came in relief for Max Lanier with one out in the sixth and runners on second and third and retired the last 11 batters in a row, including pinch-hitter Mike Chartak.

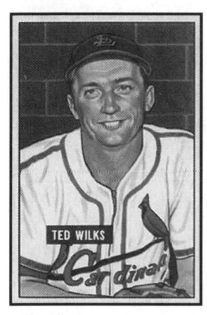

Photo by Bowman Gum; http://commons.wikimedia.org/wiki/File:Ted_Wilks.jpg

The 28-year-old Wilks struck out Chartak to get the save and to give the Cardinals their fifth world championship. With the 3-1 victory in game six, the Cardinals beat the Browns 4 games to two in the all-St. Louis World Series.

Wilks was part of a St. Louis team that cruised past the National League in the 1944 season. After losing to the Yankees in the World Series the year before, the Cardinals won a league-best 105 games and won the National League by 14.5 games. St. Louis was first in the NL in ERA and strikeouts.

Wilks began his nine-year major league career with the Cardinals in 1944 and stayed with them until 1951, when he was traded to the Pirates. He was traded the Indians in 1952 and retired after the 1953 seasons.

Wilks turned in a successful run with the Cardinals. He was 51-20 in his seven years with the team and won two World Series championships. He had an 8-0 season in

1946, and led the National League in saves (nine) and games pitched (59) in 1949.

Wilks was born on November 13, 1915 in Fulton, New York, which is outside Syracuse. Fulton was incorporated as a city just 13 years earlier.

While playing in the majors, Wilks earned the nickname "Cork" in reference for shutting down opponents. He finished with 46 saves, including a career-high 13 in 1951 with the Pirates.

Wilks died on August 21, 1989 at age 73 in Houston, Texas.

***

In 2006, another Cardinals rookie, Adam Wainwright, got the final out in the World Series against the Detroit Tigers. With runners on first and third, Wainwright struck out Brandon Inge under chilly conditions at Busch Stadium to give the Cardinals their 10th World Series title and their first since 1982.

In 1982, Wainwright was a 1-year-old living in Brunswick, Georgia, a town of over 15,000 located between Savannah, Georgia and Jacksonville, Florida. He was born there on August 30, 1981.

Wainwright attended high school at Glynn Academy in Brunswick, where he played football and baseball. Wainwright was selected by the Atlanta Braves in the first round of the 2000 amateur draft, but was traded to the Cardinals three years later.

Wainwright made his major league debut with the Cardinals in 2005. The next year, Wainwright replaced Jason Isringhausen as closer in the final months of the season and finished with three saves. He also helped the Cardinals win 83 games and the NL Central Division title by just 1.5 games over Houston.

The Cardinals knocked off San Diego in four games in the NLDS and defeated the Mets in seven games in the NLCS to advance to the World Series. Wainwright got the final out of the 2006 NLCS, striking out the Mets' Carlos Beltran with the bases loaded and St. Louis leading 3-1.

Photo by Dave Herholz, http://commons.wikimedia.org/wiki/File:Adam_Wainwright_2006.jpg

Wainwright came in relief with the Cardinals leading 4-2 in the top of the ninth in game five of the World Series. He gave up a one-out double to Sean Casey and two-out walk to Placido Polanco before facing Inge. On an 0-2 pitch, the 25-year-old Wainwright struck out Inge and the Cardinals ended their 24-year championship drought.

Wainwright was one of the Cardinals' heroes in the 2006 postseason, pitching nine games and saving four of them. His career has taken off ever since.

Wainwright was moved to the starting rotation in 2007 and won 14 games. He led the National League in wins with 19 in 2009 and won 20 games in 2010. He missed all of the 2011 season due to Tommy John surgery, forcing him to see the Cardinals win another World Series championship from the bench.

Wainwright finished with over 200 strikeouts three times, played in the All-Star Game twice and earned two Gold Glove awards.

***

The other two Cardinal pitchers who finished the World Series with a strikeout – Bob Gibson and Bruce Sutter -- were no rookies. And they're both Hall of Famers.

Gibson played all 16 seasons with the Cardinals and won 251 games with nine All-Star appearances, nine Gold Glove awards and a National League MVP award.

Gibson played in the majors for five seasons before playing in his first World Series in 1964, and he helped the Cardinals won it all. Three years later against the Boston Red Sox in the World Series, he pitched three complete games to lead the Cardinals to their eighth title.

With no runners on and two outs in game seven at Fenway Park, Gibson struck out George Scott for the final out and was mobbed by his Cardinal teammates. The Cardinals won 7-2 over the Red Sox and the Series 4 games to 3.

Gibson finished 3-0 with a 1.00 ERA and 26 strikeouts in the 1967 World Series. He pitched complete game victories in game one, four and seven, and he hit a home run in the seventh game.

Photo by Baseball Digest http://en.wikipedia.org/wiki/ File:Bob_Gibson_1962.png

The next year, Gibson pitched a 1.12 earned run average and helped the Cardinals go back to the World Series, but they lost to Detroit in seven games. Gibson turned in a memorable performance in game one, striking out a World Series record 17 batters.

Gibson won 251 games and struck out 3,117 batters in his career, earning him a spot in Cooperstown in 1981.

Pack Robert Gibson was born on November 9, 1935 in Omaha, Nebraska. Before joining the Cardinals in 1959, Gibson was once a basketball standout, earning a scholarship to play basketball in Creighton University -- which is located in Omaha -- and playing with the Harlem Globetrotters.

By 1967, Gibson was already a star pitcher for the Cardinals, winning over 100 games and playing in four All-Star games. He was 13-7 with a 2.98 ERA and 147 strikeouts despite missing nearly two months from a leg injury.

By the time Gibson returned in early September 1967, the Cardinals were cruising in the National League standings, winning 101 games and capturing the pennant by 10.5 games over San Francisco.

In the seventh game of the World Series, St. Louis scored two runs in the third, two in the fifth – including Gibson's solo home run -- and three in the sixth. In the bottom of the ninth, the 31-year-old Gibson gave up a single to Carl Yastremski, then got Ken Harrelson to ground out into a double play. Finally, he struck out George Scott to end the Series.

Gibson retired with the Cardinals in 1975.

***

Cardinal fans had to wait another 15 years for another championship. Just like Gibson in 1967, Sutter ended the 1982 Series with a strikeout. On a 3-2 pitch – after four consecutive foul balls -- Sutter struck out Gorman Thomas to help the Cardinals end their 15-year World Series championship drought.

Sutter played five seasons with the Cubs before joining the Cardinals in 1981. He also played with the Braves for three seasons. Sutter finished with 300 saves, and was inducted to the Hall of Fame in 2006.

Long before he was a World Series champion, Howard Bruce Sutter was growing up in the Susquehanna Valley area on central Pennsylvania. He was born in Lancaster, Pennsylvania on January 8, 1953. Sutter graduated from Donegal High School in Mt. Joy, which is 12 miles west of Lancaster.

Sutter was selected by the Washington Senators in the 1970 MLB Draft. The next year, after attending Old Dominion University, Sutter signed with the Cubs.

Sutter joined the Cubs in 1976. Three years later, he saved 37 games and earned his first and only Cy Young Award.

Sutter joined the Cardinals in 1981. That year, St. Louis finished with the best record in the National League East Division, but didn't make the postseason because -- due to the two-month strike -- postseason berths were awarded to the team with the best record in the first and second halves of the season, which the Cardinals didn't accomplish. They finished second in both halves of the season, so Sutter had to wait another year to play in his first postseason.

In 1982, Sutter led the National League in saves with 36 and helped the Cardinals win 92 games and the NL East by three games over the Phillies. It was St. Louis' first division title since divisional play began in 1969.

The Cardinals swept the Braves in three games in the NLCS to advance to the World Series against the Brewers. Down 3 games to 2, St. Louis rallied to win game six (13-1) and seven (6-3) at Busch Stadium to win its ninth World Series title and its first in 15 years.

The 29-year-old Sutter came in the eighth inning of game seven and retired all six batters, including Thomas, to get his second save of the Series. It was also the last World Series game Sutter pitched in.

Sutter finished with a career-high 45 saves in 1984. But the next year, he joined the Braves and stayed in Atlanta for three seasons before retiring in 1988.

***

When game seven of the 1982 World Series was on NBC-TV, Joe Garagiola, who was the play-by-play man, let the fans do the talking by not saying anything when Sutter got the strikeout.

When Thomas came up at bat, Garagiola told the audience, "The crowd will tell you what happens." After the final out, thousands and thousands stormed onto Busch Stadium to celebrate the Cardinals' World Series title, while the players were in their clubhouse soaked with champagne.

Two years earlier, Garagiola gave the audience the silent treatment when Tug McGraw struck out Willie Wilson for the final out of the 1980 World Series between the Phillies and Royals.

"The crowd will tell you what happens."

That's what Garagiola said when Tug McGraw had a 1 ball, two-strike count on Willie Wilson with two outs in the top of the ninth in game six of the 1980 World Series between the Phillies and Royals. Instead of trying to go haywire on announcing the Phillies winning the World Series, Garagiola decided to let the fans do the work in the telecast.

When McGraw struck out Wilson for the final out of the Series, Garagiola said nothing. Long-suffering Phillies fans waited all of their lives to see their team win a world championship for the first time, so Garagiola wanted to let the Phillies fans do the describing of the game for that one moment.

But getting the final out wasn't easy for the Phillies. The Royals had the bases loaded with one out and had a chance to turn in a big inning with them trailing 4-1. Kansas City needed a victory to send the World Series to a game seven for the second straight year. But thanks to a foul-ball catch by Pete Rose (with a little help from catcher Bob Boone) and the strikeout by McGraw, the Phillies kept the World Series banner in Pennsylvania. The Pirates won it all the previous year.

But this wasn't McGraw's first world title. In 1969, he helped the Miracle Mets win their first crown after finishing last place for seven straight seasons.

After striking out Wilson on October 21, 1980, McGraw gave the Phillies their first World Series championship in nearly 100 years of existence.

The Phillies were born in 1883, replacing a team for Worcester, Massachusetts in the National League. They were known as the Philadelphia Quakers, but they officially adopted the nickname "Phillies" in 1890.

The Phillies won their first National League pennant in 1915. Then, they went into obscurity, finishing with just one winning season between 1918 and 1948.

In 1950, the Phillies won their second National League pennant, and were known as the Whiz Kids because of their numerous young players. Phillies fans had to wait another 30 years to see their team in the World Series.

During that 30-year span, the Phillies blew a six-and-a half game lead and lost to the National League pennant in 1964 and won three straight NL East Division titles from 1976-78, but lost in the NLCS in all three years.

But McGraw helped the Phillies get on top for the first time. He was 36 years old when the Phillies won it all in 1980.

Frank Edwin McGraw was born on August 30, 1944 in Martinez, California. McGraw got the nickname "Tug" from his mother, Mable, because of his aggressive way of being breast-fed.

McGraw was 20 when he made his major league debut with the Mets in 1965. Four years later, he finished 9-3 with 12 saves to lift the Mets to a world title. In 1973, he came up with the rallying cry, "Ya Gotta Believe," and helped the Mets win another National League pennant, but they lost to the A's in the World Series.

After nine seasons with the Mets, McGraw went to the Phillies in 1975. In his first year at Philadelphia, McGraw played in his second and final All-Star Game. He also finished 9-6 with 14 saves.

In 1980, McGraw finished 5-4 with 20 saves. He helped the Phillies win 91 games, capture the National League East by one game over Montreal and beat Houston in five games in the NLCS.

McGraw finished 1-1 with two saves in the World Series. He picked up the save in the Phillies' 7-6 win in game one and recorded the win in relief in the Phillies' 4-3 in game five. Game six was McGraw's last World Series appearance.

McGraw stayed with the Phillies until 1984. He finished his career at 96-94 with 180 saves.

McGraw died in January 2004 after a nine-month battle with brain cancer. Country singer Tim McGraw spread his father's ashes on the pitcher's mound in Game 3 of the 2008 World Series between the Phillies and the Tampa Ray Rays.

***

Speaking of the 2008 Fall Classic, Phillies fans saw their team celebrate another world championship. Brad Lidge struck out Tampa Bay's Eric Hinske for the final out of the 2008 World Series.

Lidge helped the Phillies win their second world title and their first since 1980, when McGraw ended the World Series with a strikeout. Philadelphia topped the Rays 4-3 in game five at Citizens Bank Park to win the Series 4 games to 1.

Lidge announced his retirement after 11 seasons in the game on August 1, 2013 in Philadelphia. He said that getting the final out will live in his memory forever.

"That was a pretty fun time," Lidge said. "At first, after the pitch, I remember just saying, 'Oh, my God, we just won the World Series.' I remember Chooch (Phillies catcher Carlos Ruiz) coming out (and hugging me) and all of the sudden, it was just a complete blackout for the next couple of seconds and with large human beings jumping on top over and over and over. I watched the replay on that. I saw Shane

Victorino jumping on top, then go back and doing it again. So I know there were a lot of guys jumping on top of us.

"Chooch and I had a chance to talk a couple of days ago and we were saying, 'When we were in the bottom of that pile, neither of us could really breathe and our faces were like pushed next to each other. But we were still screaming.' It was just that feeling like it didn't matter if the weight of the world was on you or whatever because it felt like no weight was on you at the point. It was an incredible feeling that I tried to describe it but it's still indescribable. It was the greatest feeling you can have a baseball player, I believe."

Lidge celebrated his first world championship with the Phillies. He also went 7 for 7 in postseason saves after going 41 for 41 during the regular season.

Lidge began his major league career in 2002 with the Astros. The next year, he was the winning pitcher in the Astros' six-pitcher tandem that no-hit the Yankees on June 11. In 2004, Lidge became the team's full-time closer.

In 2005, Lidge saved a career-high 42 games, played in his first All-Star Game and played in his first World Series as the Astros beat the Cardinals in the NLCS. Lidge gave up a three-run homer to Albert Pujols in the game five loss at Houston, but the Astros bounced back to win game six and clinch their first World Series berth. Houston was swept by the White Sox in the Fall Classic.

Three years later, Lidge joined the Phillies and his first year in Philadelphia was a memorable one, saving 41 games, earning the NL Comeback Player of the Year award and helping his team win its second championship. The Phillies won 92 games, captured the NL East title, beat the Brewers in the NLDS and the Dodgers in the NLCS for their first pennant in 15 years.

Lidge finished with two saves in the World Series. He picked up the save in the Phillies' 3-2 win in game one. In game five, the 31-yer-old Lidge struck out Hinske with the tying run on second to clinch the Phillies' championship.

Like McGraw, Lidge also had a nickname. It's called Lights Out. He saved 225 games during his 11 seasons. Lidge stayed with the Phillies until 2011. He pitched the 2012 season with the Nationals before retiring after the season. After signing a one-day ceremonial contract on Aug. 1, 2013, Lidge officially retired as a Phillie.

Today, Lidge lives in Englewood, Colorado with his family. Born on Dec. 23, 1976 in Sacramento, California, Lidge moved to the Denver suburb at a young age. He attended Cherry Creek High School at Greenwood Village.

***

Before the Phillies won their first world title in 1980, Phillies fans had to wait 30 years for their team to get to the World Series. They hadn't played in the World Series since 1950, when they were known as the Whiz Kids.

But the New York Yankees were the smarter team in that World Series, sweeping the Phillies in four games.

Allie Reynolds ended the 1950 World Series by striking out Stan Lopata. He won the third of his six world championships with the Yankees. Known as "Superchief," Reynolds joined the Yankees in 1947 after playing with the Indians for four years. When he retired in 1954, the right-hander from Oklahoma finished with 182 wins and 1,423 strikeouts.

In the fourth game of the 1950 World Series, Reynolds came in relief for Whitey Ford with the Phillies having runners on first and second with two outs in the bottom of the ninth and the Yankees were leading 5-2. Philadelphia scored a pair of runs in that inning on an error to end the Yankees' shutout.

Stan Lopata came to pinch hit and had a chance to tie the game with a home run, but Reynolds – who picked up a 10-inning, complete-game victory in game two -- got the save by striking out Lopata.

Reynolds finished with a 16-12 record and two saves in 1950. He finished with winning seasons in all eight years with the Yankees. Reynolds won a career-best 20 games in 1952.

Reynolds was born in Bethany, Oklahoma on February 17, 1917. He played football and baseball and competed in track and field at Oklahoma Agricultural & Mechanical College (now known as Oklahoma State University).

Photo by Bowman Gum; http://commons.wikimedia. org/wiki/File:Allie_ Reynolds_1953.jpg

Reynolds signed with the Indians in 1939. Three years later, he made his major league debut. After finishing 50-47 with Cleveland, Reynolds headed to the Bronx in 1947 after getting traded for second baseman Joe Gordon. In his first season in New York, Reynolds won 19 games and helped the Yankees win the World Series.

In 1950, the 35-year-old Reynolds helped the Yankees win 98 games and the American League pennant by three games over Detroit. New York went on to win its 13th world championship.

Reynolds also helped the Yankees win it all in 1949, 1951, 1952 and 1953. After finishing 13-4 in 1954, Reynolds retired. The year before, Reynolds suffered a back injury when the Yankees' charter bus crashed into an overpass in Philadelphia, resulting in his decision to retire.

Reynolds died on December 26, 1994 at age 77 in Oklahoma City.

***

Joe Page became the first Yankee pitcher to end the World Series with a strikeout. Known as the "Fireman" and "Gay Reliever," Page struck out Gil Hodges with runners on first and second with two outs in the bottom of the ninth in game five of the 1949 World Series between the Yankees and Brooklyn Dodgers. The Yankees beat the Dodgers 10-6 at Ebbets Field to win the Series four games to one.

Page joined the Yankees in 1944 and earned an All-Star berth that same year. After eight seasons, he won 57 games with 76 saves and 519 strikeouts. During the time Page was pitching, the save was not an official statistic. It became official in 1969.

A relief pitcher is a substitute player who enters the game whenever the starting pitcher is fatigued, injured or ineffective. Back in the early days of Major League Baseball, substituting a player was not allowed except for sickness or injury.

Firpo Marberry was the first prominent reliever, pitching a total of 364 games in relief situations from 1923-1935. Johnny Murphy was another reliever who pitched for the Yankees in the 1930s and 1940s and became known as "Fireman" for his effectiveness in relief.

After World War II, full-time relievers started to become more popular. During that time, Page became a standout reliever, saving 76 games between 1946-1950. He led the American League in saves in 1949 with a career-high 27.

Page's solid performances in relief earned him the nickname "Fireman." Joe DiMaggio came up with the second nickname, "The Gay Reliever." Back then, gay meant carefree.

Page also finished the 1949 season with a 13-8 record and won the inaugural Babe Ruth Award for his performance in the 1949 World Series. He pitched in three games, finished 1-0 with the save in game five.

Page was born on Oct. 28, 1917 in Cherry Valley, Pennsylvania. He grew up in Springdale, a small town outside Pittsburgh. At age 23, Page was signed by the Yankees as an amateur free agent.

Page became a starting pitcher when he joined the Yankees in 1944. Three years later, the 31-year-old left-hander won a career-best 14 games – all in relief – and led the AL in saves with 17 and helped the Yankees win their 11th World Series championship as New York topped Brooklyn in seven.

The Yankees won 97 games in 1949 and edged Boston by one game to win the American League pennant after placing third the year before. They would go on to win the first of their five consecutive world championships.

Game five against the Dodgers in 1949 was the last World Series game Page participated in. After finishing 3-7 with 13 saves in the 1950 regular season, Page wasn't on the

Yankee roster when New York played the Phillies in the Fall Classic. The Yankees released him in 1951.

Page pitched one more season with the Pirates in 1954 before retiring. He died on April 21, 1980 in Latrobe, Pennsylvania.

***

In 1956, another Yankee pitcher ended World Series with a strikeout – this time it was Johnny Kucks. Kucks pitched a three-hit, 9-0 shutout over the Brooklyn Dodgers in game 7 of the World Series in Ebbets Field.

Photo by Baseball Digest http:// commons.wikimedia.org/wiki/ File:Johnny_Kucks_1956.png

With a runner on first, Kucks struck out Jackie Robinson for the final out of the Series. It was Kucks' only strikeout in the game. Kucks was also the last pitcher to face Jackie Robinson, and it was the last World Series game played at Ebbets Field.

Kucks pitched two innings of relief before getting the start in game seven on October 10, 1956. His gem in the final game was overshadowed by Don Larsen's perfect game in game five two days before.

The 24-year-old Kucks finished with a brilliant 1956 season, winning a career-high 18 wins with three shutouts, earning a trip to the All-Star Game and helping the Yankees win their 17th world title after losing to the Dodgers in seven games in 1955.

The Yankees advanced to the World Series by winning 97 games and capturing the American League pennant by nine games over the Indians.

Kucks was born on July 27, 1933 across the Hudson River in Hoboken, New Jersey. He played one year of minor league ball in the Yankees organization before serving in the Army.

Kucks began his major league career in 1955 with the Yankees, going 8-7 with a 3.41 ERA. He also finished with eight-win seasons in 1957 and 1958. In 1959, Kucks was traded to the Kansas City A's and finished with another eight-win season. After going 4-10 in 1960, Kucks' career ended.

Robinson's career came to an end after Kucks struck him out in the 1957 World Series. After being traded to the Giants during the off-season, Robinson decided to retire. As for the Dodgers, they moved to Los Angeles in 1958.

Kucks died on October 31, 2013 at age 80 at Saddle River, New Jersey.

***

With 27 World Series titles, the Yankees have won more championships than any other team. Out of the 27 titles, eight of them were against the Brooklyn/Los Angeles Dodgers.

The Dodgers won six World Series, two of them ended with a strikeout. In 1965, Sandy Koufax struck out Bob Allison with a runner on first and two outs in the bottom of the seventh in the seventh game of the World Series between the Dodgers and Minnesota Twins at Metropolitan Stadium in suburban Bloomington. The 29-year-old Koufax struck out 10 batters and gave up just three hits in that contest to help the Dodgers win their third world title since moving to Los Angeles in 1958.

Photo by New York Public Library Picture Collection; http://en.wikipedia.org/wiki/ File:Sandy_Koufax.jpg

Koufax joined the Dodgers organization in 1955, when they were in Brooklyn. That's where he was born on Dec. 30, 1935. He played baseball and basketball for Lafayette High School in Brooklyn.

Koufax's major league baseball career got off to a slow start, going 9-10 in his first three years with the Brooklyn Dodgers. In the Dodgers' first season in Los Angeles, Koufax finished 11-11. After finishing 8-13 in 1960, Koufax considered quitting baseball.

But Koufax stuck with it in 1961 and immediately blossomed into a standout pitcher. He led the National

League in strikeouts four times and in earned run average five times.

In 1965, Koufax finished 26-8 with a 2.04 ERA and a career-high 382 strikeouts while pitching in pain for most of the year. He pitched a perfect game against the Cubs on September 9. And he helped the Dodgers win the National League pennant after Los Angeles won 97 games and edged out the Giants by two games.

Koufax was scheduled to pitch game one of the 1965 Fall Classic against the Twins, but declined due to his observance to Yom Kippur. He pitched game two, but lost that game 5-1 and Minnesota took a 2-0 games to none lead.

The Dodgers rallied to take a 3 games to 2 lead after winning all three games at L.A. The Twins tied the Series at three after winning game six in Minnesota.

The Dodgers came out on top in game seven, beating the Twins 2-0 to win their second championship in three years. Koufax finished with a 2-1 mark with a 0.38 ERA and 29 strikeouts in the Series.

Koufax led the Dodgers to another National League pennant in 1966, but his team lost to the Orioles in the Fall Classic. He stepped down after 1966 due to arthritis in his left elbow. During his 11-year career, Koufax won 165 games, captured three National League Cy Young Awards and an MVP award.

***

By striking out Allison in the 1965 Fall Classic, Koufax became the first of seven players to make the final out and win MVP honors in the same World Series.

Orel Hershiser accomplished the same feat in the 1988 World Series against the A's. He struck out Tony Phillips for the final out in the fifth game at Oakland-Alameda County Coliseum. Hershiser finished with a 2-0 record and won Series MVP honors.

Hershiser turned in a Koufax-type season in 1988, becoming the only player to win the Cy Young Award, the National League Championship Series MVP and the World Series MVP in the same year. He also pitched a record 59 consecutive scoreless innings, breaking the old mark set by another Dodger pitcher, Don Drysdale.

Hershiser was born in Buffalo, New York on September 16, 1958. He also lived in Detroit, Toronto and Cherry Hill, New Jersey during his first 18 years of his life.

While pitching for Cherry Hill High School East, he set the single-game strikeout record with 15 in 1976 (that record was broken in 1997), and is the school's leader in career winning percentage, strikeouts and earned run average.

After playing ball at Bowling Green State University, Hershiser was selected by the Dodgers in the 17th round of the 1979 draft. Four years later, he joined the Dodgers and pitched eight games.

Hershiser, who was known as Bulldog, was 11-8 in his first full season in 1984. The next year, he led the National League in winning percentage with an .864 after going 19-3 and he helped the Dodgers win the NL West.

After finishing with .500 records in 1986 and 1987, Hershiser led the National League in wins (23), innings (267), shutouts (8) and complete games in (15) and was third in ERA at 2.26 in the 1988 season.

The Dodgers picked up 94 victories and won the NL West by seven games over Cincinnati for their fourth division title in the 1980s and their seventh overall. They beat the Mets in seven games in the NLCS to advance to the World Series against Oakland. Hershiser pitched a five-hit, 6-0 shutout over the Mets in game seven to earn MVP honors.

The Dodgers came into the 1988 World Series as underdogs, but they became the top dogs, beating Oakland four games to one for their fifth World Series championship.

"I'm just proud of this club," Hershiser told the Los Angeles Daily News on Oct. 21, 1988. "We don't have as much talent as other world champions, but we have heart and soul."

A day after Kirk Gibson hit a dramatic two-run homer in game one to lead Los Angeles to a 5-4 win, Hershiser pitched a 6-0 shutout in game two to give the Dodgers a commanding 2 games to none lead.

The Dodgers clinched the World Series title by winning 5-2 over the A's, who won 104 games. After retiring the first two batters in the bottom of the ninth, Hershiser gave up a single to Carney Lansford. Lansford later reached third, but was stranded there after the 30-year-old Hershiser struck out Phillips. Hershiser struck out nine, gave up four hits and walked four to help the Dodgers win their second World Series title in the 1980s.

Hershiser continued to play with the Dodgers until 1994. He played with the Indians from 1995-97 and played in two World Series, but Cleveland lost both of them. Hershiser pitched the Giants in 1998 and the Mets in 1999 before returning to the Dodgers in 2000 and retired after that. Hershiser is now working as an analyst for baseball games on ESPN.

***

Jesse Orosco was also on that 1988 Los Angeles team that won it all. Two years before, he helped the Mets win their second world championship. And, like Hershiser, he got the final out.

In game seven of the 1986 World Series, Orosco struck out Boston's Marty Barrett for the last out. The week before, Orosco struck out the Houston Astros' Kevin Bass for the final out of the NLCS in game six at the Astrodome.

Orosco played in his first World Series of his 16-year career in 1986. Born on April 21, 1957 in Santa Barbara, California, Orosco pitched in a major league record 1,252 games with nine different teams. His long career began with the Mets in 1979.

By then, the Mets were struggling, losing 99 games and finishing last in the National League East for the third straight season. Orosco returned to the majors in the strike-shortened 1981 season and pitched in eight games. After losing a career-high 10 games in 1982, Orosco bounced back the next year to win a career-high 13 games, plus he saved 17 games and earned the first of two trips to the All-Star Game.

In 1984, Orosco saved a career-high 31 games and helped the Mets finish with their first winning season in eight years, going 90-72 and finishing second in the NL East.

After finishing second again in 1985, the Mets came out on top in 1986, winning a franchise-best 108 games. New York advanced to its third World Series in franchise history by beating the Astros in six games in the NLCS.

Orosco finished with his fourth consecutive winning season, going 8-6 with 21 saves. He went 3-0 in the NLCS against Houston.

Boston took a 2 games to 0 lead over the Mets in the World Series before New York rallied to win the Series in seven games. Orosco retired the side in the ninth for his second save in the Fall Classic.

By striking out Barrett in the seventh game, the 29-year-old Orosco helped the Mets come back from a 3-0 deficit to win 8-5 and to hand the Red Sox another crushing defeat. Two nights before, the Red Sox were one strike away from winning the World Series, but lost 6-5 to the Mets after New York scored two runs in the bottom of the 10th on a wild pitch and the infamous "through the legs" error by Bill Buckner.

The next year, Orosco broke the 100-save mark in his career, but went 3-9 in his final season with the Mets, who finished second in the NL East for the third time in four seasons.

In 1988, Orosco went to the Dodgers, finished 3-2 with nine saves and helped Los Angeles win its fifth world title since moving to California in 1958. He would never play in another World Series.

Orosco played for the Indians (1989-91), Brewers (1992-94), Orioles (1995-99), Cardinals (2000), the Dodgers again (2001) and played Padres, Yankees and Twins in 2003 before retiring.

Orosco was drafted by the Twins in 1978 MLB Draft. He was traded to the Mets the next year for Jerry Koosman, who was on the mound for the final out of the 1969 World Series, won by the Mets. Koosman got Davey Johnson, who was managing the Mets in 1986, to fly out to left.

***

In 2004, the Red Sox ended their 86-year championship drought by sweeping the Cardinals in four games in the World Series.

Jonathan Papelbon made sure the Red Sox didn't have to wait 86 years to win another one as they won again in 2007, sweeping the Colorado Rockies in four games in the World Series.

Before joining the Red Sox in 2005, Papelbon had banner baseball careers in high school and college. Papelbon, who was born in Baton Rouge, Louisiana, attended Bishop Kenny High School in Jacksonville, Fla., and was a three-time All-City nominee. He then headed to Mississippi State, where he won nine games and saved 13 games in three years.

Papelbon made his major league debut on July 31, 2005. He began his major league career as a starter, but was moved to the bullpen in 2006 and became the team's closer. With 35 saves, Papelbon set the single-season record for most saves by a Red Sox rookie.

The next year, Papelbon saved 37 games, becoming the first Boston reliever with back-to-back 30 save seasons. He also helped the Red Sox win 96 games and the American League East Division title.

After beating the Angels in the ALDS and coming back from a 3 games to 1 deficit to beat the Indians in the ALCS, the Red Sox were back in the World Series. Like in 2004 against the Cardinals, Boston finished with a four-game sweep over Colorado.

Papelbon retired the side in the bottom of the ninth at Coors Field. He struck out Colorado's Seth Smith for the final out.

Papelbon finished with three saves in the World Series, including Boston's 4-3 victory over the Rockies in game four. As of Opening Day 2014, it's Papelbon's only trip to the World Series.

Papelbon is currently pitching with the Phillies. After heading to Philadelphia in 2012, Papelbon left Boston as the franchise's all-time leader in saves with 219.

***

Brian Wilson helped the San Francisco Giants put an end to a long drought on November 1, 2010.

That's when he struck out Texas' Nelson Cruz for the final out of the World Series in game five at the Ballpark in Arlington and helped the Giants win their first World Series title since 1954 and their first championship since moving to San Francisco in 1958. San Francisco beat the Rangers 4 games to 1.

The long-bearded, right-handed reliever took his arms and made an X before the team celebrated near the pitchers' mound. The week before, Wilson took his arms and made an X after striking out Philadelphia's Ryan Howard for the final out of the NLCS in game six at Citizens Bank Park.

So far, Wilson has one World Series championship and that came in 2010. After going through Tommy John surgery in 2012, he had to see the Giants win another World

Series championship from the bench. Wilson completed his first season with the Dodgers in 2013.

Photo by Rob Shenk ; http://en.wikipedia.org/ wiki/File:Brian_Wilson_ Fear_the_Beard.jpg

Before he started his major league career out west, Wilson was growing up in New England. He was born on March 16, 1982 in Winchester, Massachusetts, but moved to Londonderry, New Hampshire in second grade.

After playing baseball at Londonderry High School, Wilson moved south to Baton Rouge to play college baseball at LSU. He won 18 games, lost 10 and saved five. During his junior year, Wilson injured his elbow and underwent Tommy John surgery.

Wilson was picked by the Giants in the 24th round of the MLB Draft in 2003. Three years later, he joined the Giants. In his third season in 2008, Wilson became one of the top relievers, saving 41 games and earning a trip to the All-Star Game.

Two years later, Wilson was one of the key players in the Giants' championship run. He earned his second trip to the All-Star Game and led the National League in saves with 48.

Before 2010, the Giants had won just three National League pennants since moving to San Francisco in 1958. They were 0-3 in World Series play, losing to the Yankees in seven games in 1962, their Bay Area rivals A's in four games in 1989 and the Angels in seven games in 2002.

San Francisco won 92 games, captured its eighth National League West Division title and beat a pair of NL East teams, the Braves and Phillies, to advance to the World Series against the Rangers, who were playing in their first Fall Classic in franchise history.

Wilson's dark beard kept growing longer during the Giants' 2010 postseason run, forcing Giants' fans to start growing beards or wear fake beards.

The Giants won the fifth game 3-1. Series MVP Edgar Renteria hit a three-run homer in the top of the seventh to break a scoreless tie.

Cruz hit a solo home run in the bottom half of the inning to give the Rangers their only run in the game. Wilson made sure Cruz wouldn't hit another home run in the bottom of the ninth. With no runners on base, the 28-year-old Wilson struck out Cruz on a 3-2 pitch to pick up his first and only save in the World Series.

Wilson finished with 36 saves in 2011. As of Opening Day 2014, Wilson has over 170 saves.

***

In 1958, the state of California had its first major league baseball teams as the Dodgers and Giants moved out of New York City and headed to Los Angeles and San Francisco, respectively.

Then, the Los Angeles Angels of Anaheim joined Major League Baseball in 1961 as an expansion team. In 1968, the A's moved to Oakland from Kansas City. The next year, the San Diego Padres were born, giving California five baseball teams.

The California teams have a combined 12 World Series titles, with the Dodgers having the most with five. Also, California has 10 players who made the final out of the World Series, more than any other state.

Sergio Romo is one of those 10 players. When he struck out Cabrera in the 2012 World Series, Romo joined Lidge, Frankie Crosetti, Joe DiMaggio, Tug McGraw, Allen Craig, Jesse Orosco, Ken Landreaux, George "High Pockets" Kelly and Joe Gordon in a list of California players who made the last out of the Fall Classic.

Romo was born on March 4, 1983 in Brawley, located 13 miles north of El Centro, about 30 miles from the Mexico border, 70 miles west of Yuma, Arizona and 130 miles east of San Diego. Incorporated in 1908, Brawley is a leading agricultural center and has over 24,000 people.

Romo played shortstop and third base for the Brawley Union High baseball team. After graduating there in 2001, Romo went to play baseball for four

Photo by Chris Martin; http://en.wikipedia. org/wiki/File:Sergio_Romo_2010.jpg

different colleges – Orange Coast College, Arizona Western College, the University of North Alabama and Mesa State College (now Colorado Mesa University).

Romo was drafted by the Giants in the 28th round in 2005. Three years later, he made his major league debut.

Romo was part of the 2010 Giants World Series championship team as a set-up man. When Wilson was out in 2012 due to Tommy John surgery, Romo was in as the San Francisco closer.

Romo finished with 14 saves and helped the Giants win 94 games and another NL West title. He also helped the Giants turned in a remarkable postseason run, coming back from a 2 games to none deficit by beat Cincinnati in five games in the NLDS, a 3-1 hole to beat the 2011 world champion Cardinals in the NLCS and sweeping the Tigers in four games in the World Series.

Romo was brilliant in the Fall Classic against the Tigers, pitching three scoreless innings, recording three saves and striking out five, including the big one against Cabrera.

The Giants won 4-3 in game four on an RBI single by Marco Scutaro in the top of the 10th. Romo retired the side in the bottom half of the inning.

Romo didn't go back to the World Series in 2013, but he earned his first trip to the All-Star Game and finished with a career-high 38 saves.

***

And then there were the pitchers who didn't need to get a strikeout to clinch a World Series championship: Red Ruffing, Rollie Fingers, Mike Torrez, Mike Timlin, Josh Beckett and Keith Foulke.

***

In 1938, the Yankees' Red Ruffing ended one of his best pitching seasons of his career by getting the Cubs' Billy Herman to ground out back to him to record the final out of the World Series, where the Bronx Bombers won in a four-game sweep.

Ruffing won a career-best 21 games in 1938. He also led the American League in wins and shutouts (four). By the time he retired in 1947, Ruffing won 273 games and struck out 1,987 batters. He earned a trip to the Hall of Fame in 1967.

Before he became a Hall of Fame pitcher, Charles Herbert Ruffing was just a boy from Illinois. He grew up in Coalton, a small village which is 81 miles northeast of St. Louis in Montgomery County. Coalton, which now has 300 people, is known for its shaft mining operations.

Ruffing worked in the coal mines when he was a child. After losing four toes from his left foot in a mining accident when he was a teenager, Ruffing switched from outfielder and first baseman to pitcher.

Ruffing started his career in 1924 with the Boston Red Sox. He led the American League in losses in 1928 (25 losses) and 1929 (22 losses). After starting the 1930 season 0-3 at Boston, Ruffing headed to the Yankees, where he would finish 15-5 the rest of the year.

Ruffing finished with just one losing record during his 16 years with the Yankees. With 231 wins, Ruffing is still the winningest right-handed pitcher in Yankees history. He finished with four straight 20-win seasons, including the one in 1938.

That year, the Yankees breezed through their third straight AL pennant, winning 99 games and the league by 9.5 games over Ruffing's old team, the Red Sox.

The Yankees took a 3-0 second-inning lead en route to an 8-3 win over the Cubs in game four of the Fall Classic at Yankee Stadium. Ruffing pitched a complete game, giving up two earned runs on eight hits and striking out six. He also drove in the game's first run in the bottom of the second on a two-out, RBI single.

In the top of the ninth, the 33-year-old Ruffing gave up a single to Billy Jurges before getting three straight outs, including the groundout by Herman that was the final out of the World Series.

Ruffing, who helped the Yankees win six World Series titles and made six All-Star Game appearances, wrapped up his major league career in 1947 with the White Sox. He died on February 17, 1986 at age 80 in Mayfield Heights, Ohio.

***

The Oakland A's were world champions again in 1974.

This time, they didn't need seven games to win their third straight championship.

After beating the Reds and the Mets in seven games in the World Series the last two years, the A's needed just five to knock off the Los Angeles Dodgers in the 1974 Fall Classic.

Oakland defeated Los Angeles 3-2 in game five at Oakland-Alameda County Coliseum to win its third straight title and became the first team since the Yankees from 1949-1953 to win three straight world championships.

The 28-year-old Fingers made sure the Series didn't go back to Los Angeles. In game five, he not only recorded the save, but he got the final out, getting the Dodgers' Von Joshua to ground out back to him with no runners on. Fingers earned Series MVP honors by going 1-0 with two saves, including the one in game five.

Since Fingers joined the A's 1968 – the same year they moved to Oakland – he became a dominant reliever. During his eight years with Oakland, Fingers saved 136 games. He didn't become the A's main reliever until 1971.

Fingers went on to finish his baseball career with 341 saves. He also pitched with the Padres and the Brewers. Fingers earned a spot in Cooperstown in 1992.

Roland Glen Fingers was born on August 25, 1946 in Steubenville, Ohio. He didn't stay in the Ohio Valley (a three-state area that consists of Steubenville and Wheeling, West Virginia) long as his father, who was working at a steel mill, moved his family to California. Fingers attended Upland High School in Upland.

Fingers would start his major baseball career in California as he joined the newly relocated Oakland A's in 1968. The A's moved from Kansas City, where they played for 13 seasons. During his time at Oakland, Fingers grew a waxed handlebar moustache, which he still has today.

Fingers got the save in game seven of the 1972 World Series as the A's won the first of their three straight championships. He attempted to get the save in game seven of the 1973 World Series, but after giving up a run in the top of the ninth with two outs, Fingers was relieved by Darold Knowles, who became the first in baseball history to pitch in all seven World Series games.

In 1974, Fingers finished 9-5 with 18 saves and earned a trip to the All-Star Game. He helped the A's win 90 games, capture the AL West for the fourth straight year and beat Baltimore in three games in the ALCS.

In the World Series, Fingers won game one in relief and picked up the save in game four. In game five, Fingers pitched two innings of relief, and retired the side in the ninth. It was the last World Series game of Fingers' career.

Fingers went to San Diego in 1977. After four years with the Padres, Fingers joined the Brewers in 1981. He helped Milwaukee advance to the World Series in 1982, but he didn't pitch due to injury. Fingers retired in 1985.

***

After pitching four games with the A's in 1977, Mike Torrez was traded to the Yankees, where he finished 14-12 and got the final out of the World Series.

With two outs and two runners on in the top of the ninth in game six at Yankee Stadium, Torrez caught a bunt pop fly by Lee Lacy to seal the Yankees' first world title in 15 years. He also pitched a complete-game, 8-4 victory.

The last out was overshadowed by Reggie Jackson's three home run performance in that game. Before the last out was recorded, Jackson, who was playing in right field, had to get a batting helmet for security when thousands of fans were preparing to storm onto Yankee Stadium, which they did.

A year later, Torrez joined the Red Sox and was best known for giving up the infamous home run to the Yankees' Bucky Dent in the one-game playoff to decide the American League East championship.

Torrez played with eight different teams during his 17-year career. He rejoined the A's in July 1984 after being released by the Mets that same year. A month later, Torrez was released by Oakland, and finished his career with 185 wins.

Born in Topeka, Kansas on August 28, 1946, Torrez began his baseball career in 1967 with the Cardinals, who eventually won the World Series that year. Torrez stayed with the Cardinals until midseason 1971, when he was traded to the Expos. Then, he went to the Orioles in 1975 and won a career-best 20 games. The next year, Torrez headed west to Oakland, where he finished 16-12.

Torrez advanced to his first and only World Series in 1977 after the Yankees beat the Royals in five games in the ALCS. During the regular season, they won 100 games and captured the American League East championship by just 2.5 games.

The 31-year-old Torrez finished 2-0 in the Fall Classic. He pitched a complete-game, 5-3 victory over the Dodgers in game three. Game six was the last World Series game Torrez played in his career.

***

Toronto Blue Jays fans had reason to celebrate on October 24, 1992.

By beating the Atlanta Braves 4-3 in 11 innings in the sixth game of the World Series at Atlanta-Fulton County Stadium, the Blue Jays became the first team from outside the United States to win the Fall Classic. Toronto won the Series 4 games to 2.

Helping the Blue Jays make that historic feat was Mike Timlin. With Atlanta having a runner on with two outs in the bottom of the 11th, Timlin fielded a bunt by Otis Nixon, then immediately threw him out to end the game and the Series. It was Timlin's only postseason save of his career.

Timlin would get another World Series ring for Toronto in 1993 as the Blue Jays beat the Phillies in six games thanks to a walk-off home run by Joe Carter in the sixth game. Timlin also helped the Red Sox win championships in 2004 and 2007, giving him four World Series rings for his career.

The four-time World Series champion was born on March 10, 1966 in Midland, Texas. He played high school baseball for Midland High School, which won state championships in 1973 and 2001.

Timlin pitched for Southwestern University, an NCAA Division III school in Georgetown, Texas, before getting drafted in the fifth round by the Blue Jays in 1987.

Timlin turned in a solid rookie season in 1991, winning a career-high 11 games and helping the Blue Jays win their third AL East championship.

Before they became successful in the late 1980s and early 1990s, the Blue Jays were a struggling expansion team. They started play in 1977 and finished last in the AL East in their first five seasons. Toronto didn't get its first winning record until 1983, when it started a string of 11 straight winning seasons.

The Blue Jays won a franchise record 99 games and their first AL East title in 1985, but blew a 3 games to 1 lead to the Royals and lost in seven games in the ALCS. They won another division championship in 1989, but lost to the A's in the ALCS. In 1991, Toronto lost to eventual World Series champion Minnesota in the ALCS.

In 1992, the Blue Jays won another AL East crown and finally cleared the ALCS hurdle after beating Oakland in six games to advance to the World Series against the Braves, who were making their second straight Fall Classic appearance.

The Blue Jays won all four of their games by one run in the World Series.In the sixth game, Toronto took a 4-2 lead on a two-run double by Dave Winfield in the top of the 11th.

Atlanta cut the lead to 4-3 to one run after scoring a run on a groundout. Then, the 26-year-old Timlin came in relief for Jimmy Key with two outs and got the final out to give Canada something to celebrate.

Timlin was 0-2 with a save in the 1992 regular season after winning 11 games the year before.

Timlin stayed with Toronto until 1997, when he was traded to Seattle. He pitched with the Orioles (1999-2000), Cardinals (2000-2002) and Phillies (2002) before making his final stop in Boston in 2003. In his final year in 2008, Timlin set the record for the most appearances by a right-handed relief pitcher with 1,050 games.

***

Another Texas native got the final out in the 2003 World Series. Josh Beckett helped the Florida Marlins win their second world championship by fielding a ground ball hit by the Yankees' Jorge Posada, then tagging him out in front of a stunned crowd in game six at Yankee Stadium.

Beckett joined Koufax, Hershiser, Gibson, Fingers, Scott Brosius and Brooks Robinson as the only players to get the final out and win the Most Valuable Player award in the same World Series. Major League Baseball started giving out MVP awards in the Fall Classic in 1955, when the Brooklyn Dodgers' Johnny Podres won the honor, but he didn't get the final out.

Beckett was just 23 years old when he became a World Champion baseball player. He was born in Spring, Texas in the spring of 1980 -- May 15 to be exact. Located 30 miles north of Houston, Spring was growing by the time Beckett was born. Houston's suburbs began to expand to the north, and more subdivisions and residential areas opened in the Spring area. By the mid-1980s, the town had 15,000 people. Today, it has over 54,000.

Beckett played baseball at Spring High School and was selected USA Today's High School Pitcher of the Year. Instead of pitching for Texas A&M, Beckett decided to go pro. He was drafted by the Marlins in the first round of the 1999 amateur draft.

Two years later, Beckett started his major league career with the Marlins. In 2003, he finished 9-8, but earned a spot in the postseason rotation for the Marlins, who made an improbable run to the World Series championship.

Florida earned a postseason spot by winning the Wild Card. The Marlins won 91 games and finished 10 games behind Atlanta in the National League East.

Six years before, the Marlins won their first World Series championship after beating the Indians in seven games. Edgar Renteria delivered a game-winning single in the bottom of the 11th in game seven, lifting the Marlins to a 3-2 victory over Cleveland to clinch a world title in just their fifth year of existence.

The Marlins joined the Colorado Rockies as two of the National League expansion teams in the 1993 season. They lost 98 games in their first season.

The Marlins didn't get their first winning season until 1997, when they won 92 games and won a Wild Card spot. They swept the Giants in the NLDS and beat the Braves in six games in the NLCS before winning the World Series.

In 1998, the team was dismantled, resulting in a 108-loss season for the Marlins. The Fish got back to their winning ways in 2003. That year, Jack McKeon replaced Jeff Torborg as the team's manager just one month into the season.

The Marlins beat the Giants in four games in the NLDS. Then, they came back from a 3 games to 1 deficit to beat the Cubs in the NLCS. Florida won game six – with a little help from Cubs fan Steve Bartman – and game seven at Wrigley Field to advance to its second World Series.

The Marlins came back from a 2 games to 1 deficit to stun the Yankees in six games in the World Series. Florida beat New York 2-0 in the sixth game by getting a run in the fifth and another in the sixth.

Beckett, who lost game three, pitched a five-hit shutout, struck out nine and walked two in game six. He retired the side in the bottom of the ninth, getting Bernie Williams and Hideki Matsui to fly out to left, then fielding Posada's grounder and tagging him out to wrap it up.

Beckett stayed with the Marlins until 2005. In 2006, he joined the Red Sox and the following year, he won a career-high 20 games and helped Boston win the World Series. Beckett is now pitching for the Dodgers.

***

After winning it all in 1918, the Red Sox hit a World Series drought, going 86 years without a World Series championship. During those years, the Red Sox suffered seven-game losses in the 1946, 1975 and 1986 World Series. In 1986, the Red Sox were one out away from a World Series championship as they were leading the Mets 5-3 in the bottom of the 10th in game six at Shea Stadium. But the Mets came back to win 6-5 with a little help from a grounder hit by Mookie Wilson that went through Bill Buckner's legs. The Mets won game seven and their second championship two days later.

In 2004, the Red Sox returned to the Fall Classic for the first time in 18 years by miraculously coming back from a 3 games to none deficit to beat the Yankees in the ALCS. The year before, Boston lost to the Yankees in seven games in the ALCS.

The miraculous win over the Yankees carried over for the Red Sox to the World Series against St. Louis. Boston, which entered the playoffs as a Wild Card, outscored the Cardinals 24-12 in its four-game sweep. The Red Sox won 3-0 by getting a run in the first and two in the second.

Getting the save – and the final out – was Keith Foulke. Born in 1972 in Ellsworth Air Force Base, South Dakota, Foulke began his major league baseball career in 1997 with the Giants, but was traded later that year to the White Sox.

In 2003, Foulke headed back to the Bay Area, this time he joined the Oakland A's and led the American League in saves with 43 and earned the league's Relief Man of the Year honors. But his stay in Oakland didn't last long.

The next year, Foulke headed to Boston and became the Red Sox's closer. He finished with 32 saves to help the Red Sox return to the postseason.

After playing in the ALDS with the White Sox in 2000 and with Oakland in 2003, Foulke finally got to play in his first – and only -- World Series in 2004. On Oct. 27, 2004, nine days after he turned 32 years old, Foulke turned in the greatest moment of his baseball career. In game four at Busch Stadium, Foulke got the Cardinals' Edgar Renteria to ground out back to him and Foulke threw him out to give the Red Sox their sixth world championship. It was the only save Foulke got in the World Series.

Foulke played at Boston for the next three seasons. He wrapped up his career in Oakland in 2008.Out of his 194 career saves (regular season and postseason), the save in game four against St. Louis was the most memorable of them all.

"As a kid, you always dream of hitting the game-winning home run, but I'm a pitcher and I wanted to be the guy on the mound with the ball in my hand," Foulke told the Boston Herald on Oct. 28, 2004.

CHAPTER TWO: CATCHER

In the long history of the World Series, only four catchers recorded the final out of the World Series.

Here's another interesting fact: all four of these catchers – Johnny Kling, Bob O'Farrell, Bill Freehan and Thurman Munson – recorded the final out at their opponent's home field.

The first catcher to record the final out in the World Series was a pool shark named Johnny Kling of the Chicago Cubs in 1908. When he's not playing baseball, Kling was well known as an outstanding billiards player. During the early 1900s, Kling was praised by one reporter as the best pool player of any active baseball player. He ran his own pool room in his native Kansas City home.

Kling began his major league career in 1900 with the Chicago Orphans, who later changed their name to the Cubs. Kling helped the Cubs become a baseball powerhouse from 1906-1908. The Cubs lost to the White Sox in the 1906 World Series before coming back to win in 1907 and 1908. Before the 1906 season, Kling had a contract dispute and had planned on concentrating on pool instead of playing with the Cubs. Instead, he stayed with the Cubs and hit .300 in 96 games.

The Cubs were glad Kling stayed with the team. In 1908, Kling recorded the final out of the World Series against the Detroit Tigers. With two outs in the bottom of the ninth in game five at Bennett Park in Detroit, Kling fielded a ground ball hit by his counterpart, Boss Schmidt, and threw him out for the final out of the Series. Schmidt also was the last out of the 1907 World Series, also won by Chicago.

The Cubs beat the Tigers 2-0 in game five to win the series four games to one. Orval Overall pitched a three-hit shutout and struck out 10 in the fifth game.

Known as Noisy, Kling hit .276 with a career-best four home runs and 59 RBIs in 126 games in the 1908 season. He batted .250 with four hits in the World Series.

In 1909, Kling had another contract dispute with the Cubs that forced him to spend some time away from the team and compete in pool. He won the world billiards championship that year. The next year, he returned to the Cubs despite being fined $700 for not honoring his contract in 1909. Kling played two seasons with the Boston Braves and one more year with the Cincinnati Reds in 1913 before calling it quits. He was the Braves' manager in 1912.

So far, there hasn't been anything to celebrate for the Cubs since Kling caught that final out on October 14, 1908. As of Opening Day 2014, the Cubs have the longest World Series championship drought out of all of the teams with 106 years. Their last trip to the World Series was in 1945, two years before Kling died at age 71 in Kansas City. In 2003, the Cubs came within a victory from going to the World Series as they were leading the Marlins 3 games to 1 in the NLCS. But the Marlins rallied back with three straight wins – and a little help from Steve Bartman–to win the National League pennant.

***

When the Cubs won it all in 1908, they had the most championships than any other team in the National League with two. Now, that honor belongs to their biggest rivals, the St. Louis Cardinals.

In 1926, the Cardinals won the first of their 11 World Series titles by beating the New York Yankees in seven games. The Cardinals have to thank O'Farrell for that.

With the Cardinals leading the Yankees 3-2 with two outs in the bottom of the ninth at Yankee Stadium, Babe Ruth – one of the greatest home run hitters of all time -- attempted to steal second. But O'Farrell ended the game and the Series by throwing out Ruth, who walked. Second baseman Rogers Hornsby received the throw from O'Farrell and applied the tag on Ruth to get the out.

O'Farrell played in his second World Series in 1926. He was a member of the 1918 Cubs team that won the National League pennant and lost to the Red Sox in the Fall Classic.

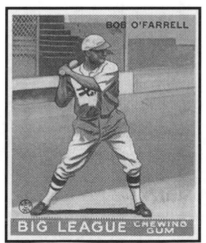

Photo by Goudey Gum Company; http://commons. wikimedia.org/wiki/ File:BobO'FarrellGoudeycard.jpg

As for the Cardinals, they played in their first World Series in 1926. Since then, they have been one of the most successful franchises in baseball.

The Cardinals' history began in 1882, when they were known as the Brown Stockings and were playing in the American Association. They later shortened their name to the Browns.

The Browns joined the National League in 1892. Seven years later, they became the Perfectos. In 1900, the team changed its current nickname to the Cardinals.

The Cardinals won 89 games and captured their first National League pennant in 1926. Between 1892-1925, the Cardinals had just nine winning seasons.

O'Farrell played in his first full season with the Cardinals in 1926. He was traded from the Cubs in the start of the 1925 season.

O'Farrell played for the Cubs for 10 years. Born in Waukegan, Illinois on October 19, 1896, Robert Arthur O'Farrell grew up a White Sox fan. When he was 10, the White Sox won their first world championship by beating the Cubs in six games. The Cubs bounced back to win back-to-back titles in 1907 and 1908.

O'Farrell signed with the Cubs in 1915. Three years later, he helped the Cubs win their first National League title since 1910.

In 1926, O'Farrell finished with an outstanding season with the Cardinals, hitting .293 with seven home runs and 68 RBIs and a career-high 30 doubles and leading National League catchers in putouts with 466 and becoming the first catcher to win the National League MVP award.

O'Farrell also hit .304 with seven hits, two runs scored and two RBIs in the World Series. He went hitless in the Cardinals' 3-2 win over the Yankees in game seven at Yankee Stadium. St. Louis won the title just nine days before O'Farrell's 30th birthday.

In 1927, O'Farrell became the Cardinals' player-manager, but the team didn't return to the World Series. After playing with the New York Giants for five years (1928-1933), O'Farrell came back to St. Louis in 1933. He played with the Reds and Cubs in 1934 before coming back to the Redbirds in 1935 and retiring after that.

O'Farrell died on February 20, 1988 at age 91 in Waukegan.

***

The Cardinals won their eighth World Series title in 1967, defeating Boston in seven games. They had a chance to win back-to-back titles for the first time in franchise history in 1968.

But Freehan spoiled the party.

Freehan, a Detroit native, helped the Tigers win their World Series title in 23 years. Detroit came back from a three games-to-one deficit to beat 1967 champ St. Louis in the World Series. Down three games to one, the Tigers won game five in Detroit and the next two in Busch Stadium.

Freehan's catch in foul territory sealed the deal. After Mike Shannon hit a solo home run with two outs in the bottom of the ninth that cut Detroit's lead to 4-1, Tim McCarver, who recently retired as the analyst for FOX Sports' baseball coverage, was at the plate.

McCarver popped up in foul territory. Freehan caught the ball. Then pitcher – and World Series Most Valuable Player -- Mickey Lolich jumped into Freehan's arms and the Tigers celebrated a World Series championship on the road.

In addition to the final out, the 26-year-old Freehan delivered a big hit in the top of the seventh. He drove Jim Northrup home on a double to left center that the Tigers a 3-1 lead. Northrup smacked a two-run triple that Cardinals center fielder Curt Flood misplayed.

The final out capped a memorable season for Freehan. He finished second to Detroit teammate Denny McLain in the American League MVP voting after finishing in the top 10 in the league in home runs (25) and runs batted in (84), and set the AL's single-season records in putouts (971) and total chances (1,050).

Freehan helped the Tigers win 103 games, a mark that was surpassed by the 1984 Tigers (104 wins). Detroit won the American League by 12 games over Baltimore.

By helping the Tigers win the World Series, Freehan helped give Detroit some spark after all the city went through the previous year. In 1967 – the year the Tigers finished second by one game to the Red Sox for the American League pennant – a riot hit the city, lasting five days and killing 43 people.

Freehan was born in Detroit on Nov.29, 1941. During that time, the city had 1.6 million people and was the leader in the auto industry, which is why Detroit is nicknamed the Motor City.

Freehan played baseball at the University of Michigan and set an all-time Big Ten Conference batting mark of .585 in 1961. He signed with the Tigers in 1961. After playing in the minors in 1962, Freehan returned to the majors to stay, and went on to turn in a successful 15-year career, all of them with the Tigers.

Freehan was an 11-time All-Star selection and a five-time Gold Glove Award winner during his 15-year tenure with the Tigers. At one point, he held the major league record for highest career fielding percentage (.9933), career putouts (9.941) and total chances (10,734). By the time he retired in 1976, he was ranked ninth in games caught (1,581), and his career totals of 200 home runs and 2,502 total bases placed him behind Yogi Berra and Bill Dickey among AL catchers.

Oh, and he was a World Series champion in 1968.

***

Also in 1968, Munson was beginning his professional baseball career. He was the fourth pick of the Major League Baseball Draft. While playing minor league baseball at Binghamton (N.Y.), Munson got to play an exhibition game against the Yankees at Yankee Stadium.

The next year, Munson was promoted to play for the Yankees, and started a 10-year major league baseball career that ended on a tragic note.

During his career, Munson was at the top of his game as Yankee catcher, winning a Rookie of the Year Award in 1970 and an American League Most Valuable Player award in 1976, playing in the All-Star Game seven times, earning three Gold Gloves and helping the Bronx Bombers win two World Series championships in 1977 and 1978, and getting the final out of the 1978 World Series.

On October 17, 1978, the 31-year-old Munson caught a foul pop fly hit by the Dodgers' Ron Cey in game six of the Fall Classic at Dodger Stadium. The Dodgers had no runners on base and two outs when Cey was at the plate.

Munson hit .320 with eight hits, three doubles, five runs scored and seven RBIs in the World Series. He hit .297 with six home runs and 71 RBIs during the regular season and played in his seventh and final All-Star Game.

Munson's final out put an end to a miraculous season for the Yankees. New York came back from a 14½-game deficit over the summer to beat Boston for the American

League East Division crown and won 100 games. Then, the Yankees beat the Royals in the ALCS for the third straight year. Finally, they came back from a 2 games to none deficit to beat the Dodgers in six games.

The Yankees clinched the World Series title with a 7-2 win over the Dodgers. It turned out to be the final World Series game for Munson.

The next year, Munson died in a plane crash while practicing takeoffs and landings with two other people at the Akron-Canton (Ohio) Regional Airport. He had been taking flying lessons for over two years and bought a plane so he could fly home to his family in Canton, Ohio on off-days.

Munson was born in Akron on June 7, 1947, but moved to Canton at age eight. He was the captain of the football, basketball and baseball teams at Lehman High School in Canton.

Munson was the Yankees' team captain from 1976-1979. During his career, Munson hit 113 home runs with 701 RBIs, 1,558 hits and a .292 batting average. It was an incredible career for a player who was gone too soon.

CHAPTER THREE: FIRST BASE

After more than 40 years, NBC wasn't going to broadcast Major League Baseball in 1990. Its last game was game five of the National League Championship Series between the Chicago Cubs and San Francisco Giants.

ABC also wasn't going to broadcast baseball in 1990 after 14 years of coverage. Its last game was game four of the World Series between the Giants and Oakland A's.

CBS took over rights for baseball coverage for the 1990 season. Jack Buck, a longtime announcer for the St. Louis Cardinals, was hired as the play-by-play man. Tim McCarver joined Buck as analyst after serving that same role for ABC for several years. Dick Stockton and Jim Kaat also were hired as the play-by-play man and analyst for alternate games.

ESPN shared baseball coverage with CBS. It was the first year the Bristol, Conn.-based cable network televised Major League Baseball. ESPN televised games on Tuesday, Wednesday, Friday and Sunday nights, but no playoff games.

CBS showed all of the postseason games, including the 1990 World Series between the A's and the Cincinnati Reds.

CBS televised a big upset in its first year of Major League Baseball coverage. The Reds stunned the powerful A's in a four-game sweep. Cincinnati won game four 2-1 in Oakland, preventing the A's from winning their second straight crown.

By catching a foul ball hit by Oakland's Carney Lansford on a 2-1 pitch from Randy Myers with two outs in the bottom of the ninth, Cincinnati's Todd Benzinger did something no first baseman had done in 53 years – making the final out of the World Series.

Benzinger was part of a Cincinnati team that went wire to wire to win its first National League West Division title since 1979 and beat Pittsburgh in six games in the NLCS. The Reds also had the "Nasty Boys" led by relievers Myers, Rob Dibble and Norm Charlton.

Benzinger played 118 games and batted .253 with five home runs and 46 RBIs in 1990. He had just two hits in the Series against Oakland in the World Series. He played in just eight seasons with five teams and hit .257 with 66 home runs and 376 RBIs.

Benzinger is one of four first basemen who made the final out of the World Series. All four of them have nicknames. Benzinger's nickname is Mercedes.

Benzinger grew up a Reds fan. He was born in Dayton, Ky., and graduated from New Richmond High School in New Richmond, 25 miles southeast of Cincy. When he was 12, he watched Cincinnati center fielder Cesar Geronimo make the final out of the 1975 World Series, forcing him to jump up so high he almost hit the ceiling of his house.

On Oct. 20, 1990, the 27-year-old Benzinger joined Geronimo, George Foster, Lonny Frey and Morrie Rath as the only Cincinnati players to make the last out of the Fall Classic.

"Every boy who plays baseball, it's his dream to catch the last out," Benzinger told the Cincinnati Post on Oct. 22, 1990. "And I did it."

Benzinger started his baseball career in 1987 with the Boston Red Sox. He helped the Red Sox win the AL East Division championship in 1988.

Benzinger joined the Reds in 1989. He led the National League in at-bats with 628. But the Reds, dealing with the lifetime banishment of manager Pete Rose, didn't make the playoffs as they finished fifth in the NL West with a 75-87 mark.

The 1990 season was Benzinger's best one. He not only played for the World Champion Reds, but he made sure they were World Champions by making the final out on that October 20, 1990 night in Oakland. Cincinnati won 91 games, captured the NL West by five games and beat Pittsburgh in six games in the NLCS to advance to the Fall Classic.

Benzinger split the 1991 season with the Reds and Royals. He also played with the Dodgers (1992) and the Giants (1993-1995).

***

Before Benzinger, the last first baseman to make the final out of the World Series was a real famous one. He was Lou Gehrig.

Gehrig made the final out of the World Series in 1936 and 1937, becoming just one of two players to make the last out of the World Series twice. The other is shortstop Everett Scott.

Gehrig was known as the Iron Horse for his durability, playing in 2,130 consecutive games, hitting .340 for his career, going to the All-Star Game seven times and helping the Yankees win six World Series, including 1936 and 1937.

Gehrig was born in New York City on June 19, 1903, the same year the World Series began and the same year the Baltimore Orioles moved to New York to become the New

York Highlanders and later the Yankees. Gehrig attended Columbia University, where he played football and baseball.

Gehrig started his major league career in 1923, the same year the Yankees won their first World Series. He saw limited time in his first two seasons, playing in a combined 23 games.

But Gehrig's playing time started to increase in 1925, and by the time the 1930s arrived, his legendary career took off.

Photo by Goudey Gum Company; http://en.wikipedia.org/wiki/ File:LouGehrigGoudeycard.jpg

In 1936, Gehrig won his third American League home run crown with 49, which matched his career-best from 1934, led the league in runs (167), walks (130) and slugging percentage (.696) and won his second league MVP award. And he also helped the Yankees return to the World Series after a three-year absence as they won the American League by 19.5 games.

Gehrig made the final out of the '36 World Series against the New York Giants by fielding a ground ball hit by Harry Danning in game six at the Polo Grounds to get the unassisted putout. Gehrig and the Yankees beat the Giants 13-5 to win the Series four games to two.

The next year, the Yankees won another league pennant. They finished with their second straight 102-win season and won the AL by 13 games.

The Yankees faced the Giants in the World Series again. And the Yankees won again, this time in five games. And again, Gehrig made the last out. With two outs in the bottom of the ninth in the fifth game, Gehrig fielded a ground ball hit by Jo-Jo White, then tossed the ball to Lefty Gomez to get the last out of the 1937 World Series. The Yankees won 4-2.

Despite leading the league in errors with 16, Gehrig turned in another outstanding offensive season in 1937, hitting .351 with 37 home runs and 159 RBIs.

Gehrig also helped the Yankees win another world title in 1938, the last World Series he participated in. He was diagnosed with amyotrophic lateral sclerosis the next year and died in 1941.

***

Gehrig wasn't the first first baseman to get the final out of the World Series. It was Jiggs Donahue of the Chicago White Sox in 1906.

The Chicago White Sox won the first of three World Series titles by beating their city rivals, the Cubs, four games to two in 1906. It was a big moment for a player who grew up in the Miami Valley area in western Ohio.

John Augustus Donahue was born in Springfield, Ohio on July 13, 1879. Springfield, which is 25 miles west from Dayton, had 12,000 people during the time Donahue was born, but now has over 60,000 people and earned an All-American City honor in 2004.

Donahue was a teenager when the Chicago White Sox began in 1894 as the Sioux City Cornhuskers of the Western League. A year later, they moved to St. Paul, Minnesota and became the St. Paul Saints.

In 1900, the Saints became the Chicago White Stockings after the Western League changed its name to the American League. That same year, Donahue began his major league career with the Pirates.

After splitting the 1901 season with the Pirates and Milwaukee Brewers (now the Baltimore Orioles), Donahue joined the St. Louis Browns in 1902. After a year off of baseball, Donahue returned in 1904 to play for the White Sox. Chicago adopted the White Sox nickname that same year.

In 1906, Donahue helped the South Siders win 93 games and the American League pennant with his strong fielding at first base. He led all AL first basemen in putouts (1,697), assists (118) and fielding percentage (.988).

Donahue also was part of the "Hitless Wonders" as he was one of just three players who hit over .250. He hit .257 with a home run and 57 RBIs.

But Donahue's hitting came to life in the 1906 World Series as he hit .333 -- which tied George Rohe for the highest batting average on the team – with six hits, four doubles and four RBIs.

Donahue's fielding became valuable in the Fall Classic, too. With the bases loaded with two outs in game six at South Side Park and the White Sox were leading the Cubs 8-3, the 27-year-old Donahue fielded a ground ball hit by Frank Schulte and recorded the unassisted putout to help the South Siders win their first world title in stunning fashion. The Cubs won 116 games, which is still a National League record.

The White Sox stormed to a 7-1 lead after two innings and never looked back in game six. Donahue drove in three runs.

Donahue led the American League first basemen in fielding percentage, assists and putouts for three straight years (1905-1907). He's No. 1 all-time among first baseman in putouts in a season with 1,846, which was accomplished in 1907.

Also in 1907, Donahue led the league in at-bats and games played, and he was among the leaders in hits and RBIs.

After five seasons with the White Sox, Donahue joined the Washington Senators in 1909 and retired after that. His life was cut short in 1914, when he died at age 34 with syphilis in Columbus, Ohio.

***

Another first baseman with a nickname got the final out of the 1921 World Series between the Giants and Yankees -- George "High Pockets" Kelly.

With one out in game eight (the World Series had a best of nine format back then), the Yankees' Aaron Ward walked. Then, Home Run Baker hit a ground ball to Johnny Rawlings and Rawlings threw it to Kelly for the second out. Ward attempted to go to third after the groundout, but the Kelly threw him out at third to complete the double play, end the game and the Series. The Giants beat the Yankees 1-0 to win the Series 5 games to 3.

Kelly played the first of his four World Series trips in 1921. He helped the Giants get to the World Series by leading the National League in home runs with 23, his only home run championship of his career. He also hit .308 and drove in 122 runs and led National League first basemen in putouts with 1,552, assists with 115 and double plays with 132.

The Giants won their ninth National League pennant in 1921. They won 95 games and edged Pittsburgh by four games to win the pennant. The Giants came back from a 3 games to 2 hole to beat the Yankees, who were making their first World Series appearance. The Giants won 1-0 on an unearned run in the first in game eight at the Polo Grounds.

The Giants won their second world title and their first since 1905. They would win three more championships before moving to San Francisco in 1958.

Speaking of San Francisco, George Lange Kelly was born there on September 10, 1895. He got the nickname "High Pockets" during his major league career because of his 6 foot, 4 inch frame.

Kelly started his major league career with the Giants in 1915 and stayed with them for two years until he was sent to Pittsburgh. After serving the military in 1918 during World War I, Kelly returned to the majors in 1919 with the Giants and turned in a successful seven-year run, winning a National League home run championship in 1921, leading the league in RBIs twice and helping his team win two world championships.

Kelly helped the Giants win another World Series in 1922. New York lost back-to-back World Series in 1923 and 1924. Kelly had seven hits in the 1921 World Series and finished with 25 in his four trips to the Fall Classic.

Kelly also played with the Reds (1927-1930), Cubs (1930) and Dodgers (1932). He retired after the 1932 season with 148 home runs, 1,020 RBIs and a .297 batting average. He was inducted to the Baseball Hall of Fame in 1973.

Kelly died on October 13, 1984 at age 89 in Burlingame, California, which is outside the San Francisco International Airport.

CHAPTER FOUR: SECOND BASE

The third time was the charm for the New York Yankees in 1923.

That year, the Yankees won the first of their 27 World Series championships after losing to the New York Giants for the last two years.

The third time was also the charm for Aaron Ward. After being the final out in the 1921 and 1922 World Series, Ward made the final out in the 1923 Fall Classic against the New York Giants by throwing out Jack Bentley on a grounder with no runners on in game six at the Polo Grounds.

The Yankees beat the Giants 6-4 to win the Series four games to two.

Since then, the Bronx Bombers added 26 more World Series titles to their trophy case, making themselves one of the most successful sports franchises in North America.

A total of 13 second basemen made the final out of the World Series, five of them were Yankees.

The 1923 season was definitely a memorable one for Ward. He not only made the final out of the World Series to give the Yankees their first world title, he also became the first Yankee player to get a hit at Yankee Stadium, which is known as the House That Ruth Built.

Ward definitely made up from what happened in 1921 and 1922. In game eight of the 1921 Fall Classic, Ward was thrown out at third after a baserunning error to end the game and the Series, which was won by the Giants five games to three. The next year, Ward flied out to the Giants' left fielder Ross Youngs for the final out in game four of the Series, which was won by the Giants four games to none.

Before he was a Yankee, Ward was a Southerner. He was born on August 28, 1896 in Booneville, Arkansas, a town of 3,990 that is located 152 miles west of Little Rock. It was incorporated in 1878, but was reincorporated in 1899, when Ward was 3 years old.

The New York Yankees were born in 1901 as the Baltimore Orioles. Two years later, they became the New York Highlanders. In 1913, the Highlanders became the New York Yankees.

Ward played 10 of his 12 major league seasons with the Yankees. He joined the Yankees in 1917, but back then the Yankees weren't a baseball powerhouse like they are now. Before they won their first American League championship in 1921, the Yankees finished with only eight winning records in their first 20 seasons of existence.

By 1921, Ward cut down on the strikeouts. In 1920, he struck out 84 times, more than any other American League batter. The next year, he cut it down to 68 times, and finished with a career-best .306.

Ward also showed he was a good fielder. He led all American League second basemen in assists in 1922 and 1923, and finished with a league best .980 fielding percentage in 1923.

In 1923, the Yankees won 98 games and the American League by 15 games over Detroit. The Yankees came back from a 2 games to 1 deficit to win their world title. In game six, the Yankees came from a 4-1 hole by scoring five runs in the top of the eighth.

In addition to getting the final out of the World Series, the 27-year-old Ward turned in a solid offensive effort, hitting a team-high .417 with 10 hits, a home run, two RBIs and four runs scored. He hit .154 in the 1922 Fall Classic and .231 in the 1921 Series.

Ward stayed with the Yankees until 1926. The Yankees returned to the World Series, but lost to the Cardinals in seven games. He didn't play in the Fall Classic.

After playing with the White Sox in 1927 and the Indians in 1928, Ward retired. He died at age 64 in New Orleans in 1961.

***

In 1943, Joe Gordon became the second Yankees second baseman to make the final out of the World Series. He also turned in an outstanding defensive effort in the World Series against the Cardinals, breaking records for putouts (20), assists (23), total chances (43) and a 1.000 fielding average.

The Yankees beat the Cardinals four games to one. In game five, New York was leading the Cardinals 2-0 with two outs in the bottom of the ninth. The Cardinals had runners on first and second before Debs Garms grounded out to Gordon for the last out of the Series. Gordon set a Series record for three assists in the eighth inning of game five.

The year before, Gordon won his first and only American League MVP award after hitting a career best .322 with 18 home runs and 103 RBIs. But his efforts didn't help the Yankees win the World Series as they lost to the Cardinals in five games.

In 1943, the Yankees headed back to the World Series by winning 98 games and the American League pennant by 13.5 games over the Senators. In the fifth game of the Fall

Classic at Sportmans' Park in St. Louis, the Yankees scored two runs in the sixth and went on to clinch their 10ᵗʰ world championship.

The 28-year-old Gordon hit just .235 in the Series, but he got a big hit in game one at Yankee Stadium– a solo home run that gave the Yankees a 2-1 lead (New York went on to win 4-2). Gordon hit four home runs in World Series play.

Gordon also helped the Yankees win it all in 1941, 1938 and 1939. When the Yankees won in 1943, they became the first major league team with 10 World Series titles.

Gordon was born in Los Angeles in 1915, but grew up in Oregon. He played baseball, football, soccer and competed in gymnastics and track and field at the University of Oregon. After playing baseball for the Ducks for two years, Gordon signed with the Yankees in 1936.

Gordon joined the Yankees in 1938 and stayed with them until 1943. He took a couple of years off while serving in the Army during World War II. Gordon returned for one more season with the Yankees in 1946 before heading to Cleveland to play for the Indians from 1947-1950. He helped the Indians win their second world title in 1948.

Gordon hit 253 home runs and drove in 975 runs and played in nine All-Star games, including the one in 1943 in Philadelphia. He managed four teams, including the expansion Kansas City Royals in their first season in 1969.

Gordon died in 1978 at age 63 in Sacramento, California. Gordon was inducted into the Baseball Hall of the Fame by the Veterans Committee in 2009. That same year, Robinson Cano became the fifth Yankee second baseman to make the final out of the World Series.

***

Cano fielded a grounder by the Phillies' Shane Victorino and threw him out in game six of the Fall Classic at Yankee Stadium, helping the Yankees win their 27th World Series title and their first since 2000. The Yankees also prevented the Phillies from winning their second straight crown.

Cano has been valuable for the Yankees since joining the team in 2005, earning two Gold Gloves, playing in five All-Star games and winning a Home Run Derby in 2011. He hit .309 with 204 home runs and 822 RBIs and 1,649 hits as of Opening Day 2014.

Cano helped the Dominican Republic win the World Baseball Classic in 2013. Cano earned MVP honors in the Classic after batting .469 with 15 hits and helping the Dominican Republic become the first undefeated team in the tournament's history.

Cano was born on Oct. 22, 1982 in San Pedro de Marcoris, Dominican Republic. He was named after baseball legend Jackie Robinson.

In 2009, the 27-year-old Cano hit .320 with 25 home runs and 85 RBIs and a career-high 204 hits. Cano helped the Yankees win 103 games, capture the AL East by eight games over the Red Sox and beat the Twins in the ALDS and the Angels in the ALCS to advance to their first World Series in six years.

The Yankees bounced from a 6-1 loss in game one to beat Philadelphia in the World Series. New York stormed to a 4-1 lead after three innings as Series MVP Hideki Matsui hit a two-run homer in the second and a two-run double in the third.

Cano played in his first World Series in 2009. Cano became the first Yankee second baseman to make the last out of the World Series since 1962, when Bobby Richardson recorded probably one of the best endings in World Series history.

Cano currently plays for the Seattle Mariners.

***

With runners on second and third with two outs and trailing the Yankees 1-0 in the bottom of the ninth of the 1962 World Series, the San Francisco Giants were attempting to do something they haven't done in 40 years – beat the Yankees in the World Series.

When they were playing in New York, the Giants beat the Yankees in the Fall Classic back-to-back years in 1921 and 1922. Then, the Yankees beat the Giants four times in 1923, 1936, 1937 and 1951.

Willie McCovey was looking to help the Giants put an end to that streak as he facing Ralph Terry at the plate. Felipe Alou, who started the ninth with a single, was at third and Willie Mays was at second after doubling off Terry.

McCovey was also looking to become the second player in three seasons to end the World Series with a hit. In 1960, Bill Mazeroski hit a game-winning home run off Terry in the bottom of the ninth to lift Pittsburgh to its first world championship since 1925.

But the 27-year-old Richardson spoiled the party, catching McCovey's line drive to end the game, the Series and the Giants' hopes of winning their first world title since moving to San Francisco four years before.

Had McCovey's line drive been about three feet higher, Richardson wouldn't have celebrated his third World Series championship. But the catch capped Richardson's best season in the majors. He hit .302 with eight home runs and

59 RBIs and an American League best 209 hits, played in the All-Star Game and won his second Gold Glove.

Richardson didn't win another World Series title after that famous catch that broke the hearts of Giants' fans. He played in two more World Series in 1963 and 1964, but the Yankees lost both of them.

In the 1964 World Series, Richardson tied a World Series record with 13 hits, but he was the final out of the Fall Classic as he popped up to Cardinals second baseman Dal Maxvill

Photo by Major League Baseball/New York Yankees; http://en.wikipedia.org/wiki/ File:Bobby_Richardson_1963

for the last out in game seven in St. Louis. The Cardinals won 7-5 to win the Series four games to three.

Richardson's final out in the 1962 World Series was his most famous defensive play of his career. He also showed the Giants how defensively strong he is. Throughout his career, Richardson won five Gold Gloves from 1961-65. He had an all-time fielding percentage of .979.

Richardson, who was from Sumter, South Carolina, played 11 years in the majors, all of them with the Yankees. He's the only player from a losing team to win a World Series MVP Award. Richardson won MVP honors in 1960 even though his Yankees lost to the Pirates in seven games.

In 1962, Richardson and the Yankees returned to the World Series after winning 96 games and capturing the American League title by five games over Minnesota. New York won the seventh and deciding game of the World Series 1-0.

By catching that line drive hit by McCovey, Richardson was the first Yankee second baseman in 15 years to record the final out of the World Series.

***

Like 1962, the 1947 World Series also went to seven games. The Yankees beat the Brooklyn Dodgers 5-2 in the final game at Yankee Stadium, which was ended on a double play.

Photo by Bowman Gum; http://commons.wikimedia.org/wiki/File:Snuffy_Stirnweiss

Second baseman Snuffy Stirnweiss turned in the second half of the double play to end the game and the Series. With one out in the top of the ninth, Brooklyn's Bruce Edwards grounded to the Yankees' Phil Rizzuto. Rizzuto tossed the ball to Stirnweiss to force out Eddie Miksis for the first out. Then, Stirnweiss threw the ball to first to get the final out to celebrate his second world championship. He also helped the Yankees win it all in 1943 and 1949.

George Henry Stirnweiss was born in New York City on October 26, 1918. Before starting his major league baseball career in 1943 with the Yankees, Stirnweiss was an all-American halfback for the University of North Carolina and drafted by the Chicago (now Arizona) Cardinals in 1940.

But Stirnweiss decided to switch from the gridiron to the diamond. In his rookie season, he helped the Yankees become the first major league team with 10 World Series championships. He led the American League in hits, triples, runs scored and stolen bases in 1944 and 1945, and won the league's batting crown in 1945 with a .309 average.

In 1947, the 28-year-old Stirnweiss helped the Yankees get back on top after a three-year hiatus. New York came back from a 2-0 deficit to beat Brooklyn in the seventh game at Yankee Stadium. A leadoff hitter, Stirnweiss had seven hits with three runs scored and three RBIs in the Series against the Dodgers and drew three walks in the seventh game.

Stirnweiss stayed with the Yankees until 1950, when he was traded to the St. Louis Browns. He then played his final two years with the Indians.

In 1958, Stirnweiss was killed at age 39 when the passenger train he was on plunged off the Newark Bay Bridge.

***

The Cardinals are second to the Yankees for the most World Series titles with 11. They're also second to New York for the most second basemen making the last out of the World Series with three. As of Opening Day 2014, DalMaxvill, Red Schoendienst and Jimmy Brown are the only St. Louis second basemen to make the last out.

By catching Richardson's pop fly in game seven of the 1964 World Series, Maxvill won the first of his four World Series championships. He also helped the Cardinals win it again in 1967 and the Oakland A's capture titles in 1972 and 1974.

The Cardinals beat the Yankees 7-5 in game seven of the 1964 World Series for their first title in 18 years. Bob Gibson, the Series' MVP, gave up solo home runs to Clete Boyer and Phil Linz before getting Richardson to pop up to Maxvill for the final out.

Charles Dallan Maxvill was born on February 18, 1939 in Granite City, Illinois, a steel town located just 10 minutes from St. Louis.

After graduating from Washington University with a degree in electrical engineering, Maxvill signed with the Cardinals in 1960. He joined the Cardinals in 1962.

In 1964, Maxvill played in just 37 games during the regular season, but played in all seven games in the World Series. Maxvill and the Cardinals advanced to the Fall Classic by the winning the National League title by one game over the Reds and Phillies. Philadelphia was in first by six and a half games with 12 games to play before collapsing.

Maxvill had just four hits in the World Series, but delivered a big hit in game seven. With one out in the bottom of the fourth, the Cardinals took a 2-0 lead with Tim McCarver stealing home and Mike Shannon stealing second. Then, Maxvill smacked a single that scored Shannon to increase the lead to 3-0. It was Maxvill's only RBI in the Series.

By making the final out, the 25-year-old Maxvill helped the Cardinals hand the Yankees their second straight World Series loss, making it the first time since 1921-22 the Bronx Bombers lost back-to-back World Series.

Maxvill stayed with the Cardinals until 1972, when he was traded to the A's. He joined the Pirates in 1973, but was traded back to Oakland in 1974 and retired after the 1975 season.

Maxvill became the Cardinals' general manager in 1984 and served that role for 10 years. During his run as GM, the Cardinals won National League championships in 1985 and 1987.

***

Schoendienst remains a fan favorite for the Cardinals. Today, he's a special assistant coach for the Cardinals.

Schoendienst turned in a solid major league career, playing for 19 seasons with the Cardinals, New York Giants and Milwaukee Braves. He was a 10-time All-Star and played on two World Series championship teams, including the 1946 World Series, which featured the famous "Mad Dash For Home" by Enos Slaughter.

Photo by Bowman Gum; http://commons. wikimedia.org/wiki/ File:Red_Schoendienst.jpg

Slaughter scored from first on a double by Harry Walker in the bottom of the eighth of the seventh game to give the Cardinals a 4-3 lead over the Boston Red Sox at Sportsman's Park.

But Boston was threatening with two outs in the top of the ninth. The Red Sox had runners on second and third and Tom McBride came in to pinch hit for Boston pitcher Earl Johnson. McBride grounded to Schoendienst, who threw the ball to shortstop Marty Marion to force out Bobby Doerr at second to end the game and the Series. Schoendienst also had two hits and a RBI while batting leadoff for St. Louis.

Schoendienst was just in his second season in the majors when the Redbirds won it all in 1946. He hit .281 with 34 RBIs, led National League second basemen with a .984 fielding percentage and earned his first trip to the All-Star Game after stealing a league-high 26 bases the year before.

Albert Fred Schoendienst was born on Feb. 2, 1923 in Germantown, Illinois, which is 41 miles east of St. Louis. At age 19, he signed with the Cardinals as an amateur free agent, and played in the minors for several years before joining the Cardinals in 1945.

In 1946, Schoendienst helped the Cardinals win their eighth National League pennant. St. Louis won 98 games and edged Brooklyn by two games in the league standings.

The Cardinals beat Boston 4 games to 3 in the 1946 World Series. By getting the final out of the World Series, the 23-year-old Schoendienst helped the Cardinals hand the Red Sox their first World Series loss. He hit .233 with seven hits and three runs scored in the Series.

Schoendienst remained with the Cardinals until 1956, when he was traded to the New York Giants. The next year, the Giants traded Schoendienst to the Milwaukee Braves, where Schoendienst helped them win the World Series. In 1958, the Braves lost to the Yankees in the World Series, and Schoendienst was the final out after flying out to center fielder Mickey Mantle.

Schoendienst returned to the Cardinals in 1961. He retired as a player two years later. Schoendienst became the team's manager in 1965, and led them to a World Series title in 1967.

Schoendienst was inducted to the Hall of Fame in 1989.

***

Brown became the first Cardinal second baseman to make the last out of a World Series when he fielded a groundout hit by the Yankees' George Selkirk in game five of the 1942 World Series at Yankee Stadium. The Cardinals beat the Yanks 4-2 to win the Series four games to one and capturing their fourth world title.

Brown was also solid at the plate in the Series, hitting a team-best .300 with six hits and an RBI. He had two hits while batting leadoff in the fifth game.

The Cardinals scored two runs in the top of the ninth to break a 2-2 tie. With the Yankees having a runner on first and two outs in the bottom of the ninth, Selkirk came in to pinch hit for pitcher Red Ruffing and he represented the tying run. But in his only at-bat in the Fall Classic, Selkirk grounded out to the 32-year-old Brown for the last out.

Brown played in his first and only World Series in 1942. He helped the Cardinals get there by hitting .256 with a career-high 71 RBIs and a league-leading 606 at-bats.

The Cardinals won their first National League pennant in eight years after winning a franchise-record 106 games and edging Brooklyn by two games in the league standings.

Brown joined the Cardinals in 1937, hitting .276 with nine triples and stole 10 bases while playing 138 games. Brown led the National League in at-bats with 645 in 1939 and hit a career-best .306 in 1941.

After playing 34 games with the Cardinals in the 1943 season, Brown was enlisted in the U.S. Army Air Forces during World War II. He returned to baseball in 1946 with the Pirates but was released after the season and retired after that.

Before he was a star for the Cardinals in the 1942 World Series, Brown was growing up in North Carolina. He was born on April 25, 1910 in Jamesville, which is located on the eastern part of the state. Brown played college baseball at North Carolina State.

Brown died in 1977 at age 67 in Bath, which was founded in 1705 and is North Carolina's oldest town.

***

The Reds won their first World Series championship in 1919 in the famous "Black Sox Scandal." Making the last out was second baseman Morrie Rath, who had a six-year hiatus from the majors before returning in 1919.

Fifty years before, the Cincinnati Reds became the first professional baseball team. They were originally known as the Cincinnati Red Stockings.

The next year, the Red Stockings lost many of their players and their namesake. Boston adopted the Red Stockings name in 1871 (that squad is now known as the

Atlanta Braves). A new Cincinnati Red Stockings team was formed in 1876, when it joined the National League. But it was expelled from the league in 1880 for violating rules such as serving beer at games and using their park to be played on Sundays.

A third Cincinnati Red Stockings team was formed in 1881 as a member of the American Association, which was a rival to the National League. The Reds won the American Association title in 1882. In 1890, the Red Stockings left the AA to join the National League and became the Cincinnati Reds.

The Reds didn't win their first National League pennant until 1919, when they finished with 96 victories and won the league by nine games over the New York Giants.

Rath joined the Reds in 1919. Ten years before, he started his major league career in the same city he grew up – Philadelphia. Rath was born on Christmas Day, 1886, in Mobeetie, Texas, a small town located in the Texas Panhandle. (Today, the town has just 107 people). But he later moved to a way bigger city called Philadelphia.

Rath joined the Philadelphia Athletics in 1909, but was traded to the Cleveland Naps (now Indians) in 1910. Rath was drafted by the White Sox in 1911, and became the team's second baseman. He was sent to the minors in 1913 and stayed there until 1917.

Rath joined the Navy in 1918, forcing him to miss the entire baseball season. But he returned to baseball the next year as a new player for the Reds.

Rath became a solid addition for Cincy, leading National League second basemen in putouts (345), assists (452) and double plays turned (59). He also finished with 13 doubles and 29 RBIs, both career bests.

The Reds beat the White Sox 5 games to 3 in the best-of-nine World Series. Rath finished with seven hits and five runs scored in the eight games. He was hit by a pitch by Chicago White Sox pitcher Eddie Cicotte, signaling a fix by the White Sox in the Series.

Cincinnati cruised to a 10-5 win over the Chicago in game eight at Comiskey Park. With two outs in the bottom of the ninth, the White Sox had runners on second and third before "Shoeless" Joe Jackson, one of the eight Chicago players responsible in the scandal, grounded out to the 32-year-old Rath for the final out of the Series.

Rath hit .267 with two home runs and 28 RBIs in his final year in the majors in 1920. He then played in the minors at Seattle and San Francisco before ending his playing career. Rath committed suicide in Upper Darby, Pennsylvania in 1945.

***

After winning their first championship in 1919, the Reds had to wait another 20 years to return to the World Series. In 1939, Cincinnati won 97 games and captured its second National League pennant, but was swept by the Yankees in the World Series.

The next year, Lonny Frey made sure the Reds weren't going to lose another World Series. Frey, who injured his foot five days before the Series against the Tigers began, made the final out by fielding a grounder hit by Earl Averill with two outs and no runners on in game seven at Crosley Field.

The Reds won 2-1 over the Tigers for their second world title, but it was Frey's first world championship. Thirty years before, he was born Linus Reinhard Frey in St. Louis.

Frey started his major league career in 1933 with the Brooklyn Dodgers. He joined the Cubs in 1937. After a year in the Windy City, Frey headed to the Queen City.

In 1940, Frey led all National League second basemen in putouts (366), assists (512) and double plays (111), just like Rath did 21 years earlier. He also led the league in stolen bases with 22 and scored a career-best 102 runs.

The Reds won 100 games, the first time they accomplished that feat. They came back from a 3 games to 2 deficit to beat the Tigers in the World Series. Five days before the World Series, Frey dropped the iron lid of the dugout water cooler on his foot. Eddie Joost replaced Frey at second base for most of the series.

Frey played in three games and got a couple of at-bats. He came in as a pinch runner for Ernie Lombardi – who was pinch hitting for Joost -- in the bottom of the seventh. Frey came in to play second in the top of the eighth, giving him the opportunity to make the final out of the series.

Known as Junior, Frey missed the 1944 and 1945 seasons due to World War II. He played another season with the Reds in 1946, then he split the 1947 season with the Cubs and Yankees. He picked up another World Series ring as the Yankees beat the Dodgers in the Fall Classic. After splitting 1948 with the Yankees and New York Giants, Frey retired.

Frey was inducted into the Reds' Hall of Fame in 1961 – the same year the Reds won their fourth National League pennant -- and in 1969, he was selected as the Reds' all-time second baseman during the team's 100th anniversary in the majors. Frey died in 2009 in Couer d'Alene, Idaho at age 99.

***

The White Sox won their second title in 1917, beating the New York Giants in six games. Eddie Collins, who went on to turn in a Hall of Fame career that included a major league record 512 career sacrifice bunts, 187 triples, 3,315 hits, 1,821 runs scored and 744 stolen bases, made the final out in game six, fielding a grounder hit by Lew McCarty and throwing him out.

To date, Collins is the only player who played for two teams with at least 12 seasons each. Known as "Cocky", Collins played for 13 seasons with the Philadelphia A's and 12 for the White Sox.

Collins was born in Millerton, N.Y. in 1887, just 12 years after the village – which is located 97 miles north of New York City -- was incorporated. After graduating from Columbia University, Collins's dream of playing baseball came true in 1906, when he joined the A's. He helped Philadelphia win World Series titles in 1910, 1911 and 1913.

Collins joined the White Sox in 1915 after declining a five-year deal to play for the Philadelphia A's. A's manager Connie Mack sold Collins to Chicago for $50,000. The White Sox paid Collins $15,000 in 1915, making him the third highest paid player in the league. Collins drew an American League-high 119 walks in 1915.

In 1917, Collins helped the White Sox win a franchise record 100 games and the American League pennant. It was the only season the White Sox finished with 100 wins or more.

Collins hit .289 with 67 RBIs, making it the first time in nine years he hit under .300. He led the American League second baseman in putouts with 353. But on Oct. 15, 1917, Collins made the biggest putout of the season.

With the White Sox leading the Giants 4-2 in the sixth game at the Polo Grounds, McCarty represented the tying run when he came in to pinch hit for Giants pitcher Pol Perritt with two outs and a runner on second, but he grounded out to the 30-year-old Collins and the Giants' hopes for their first world title since 1905 came to an end.

The White Sox captured their second World Series championship in 1917. They won another American League pennant two years later, but lost to the Reds in eight games.

Collins was part of the "Black Sox" team in 1919 that threw the World Series to the Reds, but he wasn't accused of being part of the scandal. He was the White Sox player-manager for three years (1924-26).

Collins was player-coach for the Philadelphia A's for four seasons before wrapping up his career in 1930. Collins was inducted to the Hall of Fame in 1939.

Collins died on March 25, 1961 at age 63 in Boston.

***

In 1918, the Red Sox won their third championship in four seasons with four games to two win over the Cubs. Boston won game six 2-1 at Fenway Park. Pitcher Carl Mays retired the side in the top of the ninth to clinch the championship for the Red Sox, but it was second baseman Dave Shean who recorded the final out. He fielded a ground ball hit by Les Mann and threw him out.

Shean was born not far from downtown Boston on July 9, 1883. He was born in Arlington, six miles northwest of Boston. Incorporated in 1807, Arlington was named in honor of those who were buried at Arlington Memorial Cemetery. A town of over 42,000 people, Arlington grew by over 90 percent during the 1920s.

After graduating from Fordham University, Shean began his baseball career in 1906 with the Philadelphia A's. After a year off, Shean returned to baseball in 1908 and played with the Philadelphia Phillies. He split the 1909 season with the Phillies and the Boston Braves, giving him a chance to play baseball near his hometown. In 1911, Shean headed to the Cubs. The next year, he went back to the Braves. After a four-year hiatus, Shean returned to baseball in 1917 to play for the Reds. In 1918, Shean joined the Boston Red Sox, who back then were one of the powerhouses in baseball, winning four World Series titles and losing none.

The Red Sox were a perfect fit for the 35-year-old Shean. He set career best season marks in batting average (.264), runs scored (58) and doubles (16) and finished with an American League best 36 sacrifice hits. He also helped the Red Sox pick up 75 victories and win the American League by 2.5 games over the Indians.

The 1918 World Series was played in early September due to the World War I "Work or Fight" order that prematurely ended the regular season. It was the first and only World Series Shean played in.

Shean wrapped up his career in 1919 with the Red Sox, getting just 14 hits in 29 games played. He died in 1963 in Boston after suffering injuries from a car accident.

***

What a difference a year can make for Tony Phillips.

In 1988, the Oakland A's second baseman struck out for the final out of the World Series against the Los Angeles Dodgers.

The next year, Phillips was a World Series champion for the first time as the A's swept the San Francisco Giants in four games in the earthquake-interrupted World Series. And he made the final out.

With the A's leading the Giants 9-6 with two outs and no runners on in the bottom of the ninth at Candlestick Park, the 30-year-old Phillips fielded a ground ball hit by left-handed hitter Brett Butler and tossed it to Oakland reliever Dennis Eckersley for the final out. The A's won their first world title in 15 years and their fourth since moving to Oakland in 1968.

Keith Anthony Phillips was born on April 25, 1959 in Atlanta, Georgia. He played baseball and other sports at Roswell High in Roswell, an Atlanta suburb. When Phillips was a teenager, the A's were the dominant team in baseball, winning three straight world championships from 1972-1974. But they fell into a drought into the late 1970s, finishing with three straight losing seasons.

Billy Martin was hired as manager in 1980 to help turn the A's around. Oakland got back to its winning ways that year, finishing second in the AL West with 83 wins. In the strike-shortened 1981 season, the A's advanced to the ALCS against the Yankees after beating Kansas City in the AL West Division Series.

Phillips joined the A's in 1982, but Oakland slumped to a 94-loss season and Martin was out as manager. Phillips didn't celebrate his first winning season until 1988, when the A's won 104 games and captured their first American League pennant in 14 years, but they were upset by the heavy underdog Dodgers in the World Series.

The next year, Phillips hit four home runs and drove in 47 runs and batted .262 to lead the A's to another American League pennant. Oakland won 99 games.

The A's took a 2 games to 0 lead in the all-Bay Area World Series against the Giants. But before game three, an earthquake struck the San Francisco area, delaying the World Series for 10 days before resuming on October 27. Oakland won game three 13-7 and game four 9-6 to complete the four-game sweep.

Phillips finished with four hits in the Series. He hit a solo home run in the third game and an RBI double in the fourth.

Phillips played with five different teams in a span of eight years before returning to the A's for his final season in the majors in 1999. He played for the Tigers (1990-94), Angels (1995 and 1997), White Sox (1996-97), Blue Jays (1998) and Mets (1998).

CHAPTER FIVE: THIRD BASE

Scott Brosius is a champion – again.

This time, he's a head coach of a college baseball championship team. On May 28, 2013, he coached the Linfield College baseball team to an NCAA Division III national championship. The Wildcats beat Southern Maine 4-1 in the championship game at Appleton, Wis., for their first national title in school history.

Long before he became head coach of Linfield Wildcats, Brosius helped the New York Yankees become a powerhouse. After six years at Oakland, Brosius joined the Yankees in 1998 and helped them win three straight World Series championships.

The 1998 season proved to be a memorable one for Brosius. He hit .300 with 19 home runs and 98 RBIs, played in his first and only All-Star Game at Denver and helped the Yankees win a World Series championship and earn the Series MVP honors.

Oh, and he got the final out of the Series.

With nobody on and two outs in the bottom of the ninth and the Yankees were leading the Padres 3-0 at San Diego's Qualcomm Stadium, the 32-year-old Brosius fielded a ground ball hit by San Diego's Mark Sweeney and threw him out to end the Series and give New York its 24th world title.

"It's interesting because from my first day of spring training in 1998 after my trade to the Yankees, I finished every ground ball session with "2 outs, bottom on 9th, to win the World Series". After coming from the last place A's to a team with a chance to win, I just enjoyed trying to imagine the last out," Brosius said. "So when the last out actually came my way, I had practiced it about 200 times already."

As of Opening Day 2014, Brosius was the last third baseman to record the final out of the World Series.

"Making the last throw and knowing we had won the Series was for me just pure elation, a dream come true," Brosius said. "As a kid I always dreamed about winning a World Series, so to live it was pretty special. I also joke that the real reason I got so excited was because I didn't airmail the last throw and force the game to continue with an error!"

Brosius is one of eight third basemen to get the final out of the World Series. In 1996, another Yankee, Charlie Hayes, caught the final out in the Series against Atlanta. The others are Baltimore's Brooks Robinson, Minnesota's Gary Gaetti, Eddie Mathews of the Milwaukee Braves, Charlie Deal of the Boston Braves, Hank Thompson of the New York Giants and Home Run Baker of the Philadelphia Athletics.

In addition to the final out in 1998, Brosius did pretty well at the plate, belting two home runs – both of them came in game three – and driving in six runs and getting eight hits and finishing with a .471 batting average.

Brosius also helped the Yankees turn in one of the best regular seasons in major league history. The Bronx Bombers won 114 games, two wins shy of the record set by the 1906 Cubs and the 2001 Mariners.

Brosius went on to play in the World Series three more times before retiring after the 2001 season. The Yankees won in 1999 and 2000, but lost to Arizona in seven games in 2001.

Then, Brosius returned to his alma mater, Linfield College, as assistant coach of its baseball team. In 2007, Brosius became the school's head coach, while his predecessor, Scott Carnahan, became the school's athletic director.

During his six seasons as Linfield coach, the Wildcats won over 200 games and placed in the top five in the national tournament three times, including the first place finish in 2013.

Linfield College is a private school of an enrollment of 1,600 located in McMinnville, Oregon, just 41 miles south of Portland. Brosius grew up in the Portland area before becoming a major leaguer.

Brosius was born on August 15, 1966 in Hillsboro, which is located 22 miles west of Portland. He grew up in Milwaukie, a suburb just 10 minutes south of downtown Portland.

Brosius played baseball for three years at Linfield before getting selected by Oakland in the 20th round of the amateur draft. He set school records in at-bats, hits and RBIs in his junior year at Linfield.

Brosius joined the A's in 1991. He was traded to the Yankees in 1998, where he had his best major league season. He batted .300 with 19 home runs and 98 RBIs and played in his first and only All-Star Game in Denver.

Brosius helped the Yankees win World Series titles in 1999 and 2000. He was back in the Fall Classic in 2001, but the Yankees lost to Arizona in seven games. Brosius retired afterwards, becoming assistant coach at Linfield for five years before getting the head coaching job in 2007.

***

When Hayes caught Mark Lemke's pop fly in foul territory in the game six of the 1996 World Series, he helped the Yankees end a drought. By beating the Braves four games to two, New York won its first world title since 1978. Since 1996, the Yankees won five World Series championships, more than any other team.

Hayes was growing up in Hattiesburg, Mississippi when the Yankees pulled off back-to-back championships in 1977 and 1978. He played for the Hub City baseball team that advanced to the Little League World Series in 1977, but lost in the first round.

Founded in 1882, Hattiesburg got the nickname "Hub City" after the city became the center of the lumber and railroad industries. It's also the home of the University of Southern Mississippi.

Hayes was born in Hub City on May 29, 1965. At age 18, he was drafted by the Giants in the 1983 MLB Draft. Hayes made his major league debut five years later.

For the next eight years, Hayes played for four different teams. He played for the Phillies (1989-1991), Yankees (1992), Rockies (1993-94) the Phillies again (1995), Pirates (1996) and Yankees again (1996-97).

On Aug. 30, 1996, Hayes was traded to the Yankees from the Pirates and hit .284 over 20 games to earn a spot on the postseason roster. He helped the Yankees win 92 games, capture the American League East Division title by four games, beat Texas in the ALDS and the Orioles in the ALCS and come back from a two games to none deficit to beat the Braves in the World Series.

New York won game six 3-2 at Yankee Stadium. The Braves had runners on first and second with two outs after trimming the Yankees' lead to one run on a RBI single by

Marquis Grissom. On a 3-2 pitch from Series MVP and Yankee reliever John Wetteland, Lemke popped up to the 31-year-old Hayes, ending the Braves' hopes of winning their second straight World Series title.

Hayes celebrated his first only World Series title after making that catch. He helped the Yankees return to the postseason the next year, but they lost to the Indians in the ALDS.

Hayes played with the Giants in 1998 and 1999, the Brewers in 2000 and Astros in 2001 before retiring. He participated in the Yankees' Old Timers' Day for four straight years from 2009-2012.

***

Before the Braves moved to Atlanta in 1966, the franchise won a World Series title at Boston in 1914 and Milwaukee in 1957.

The Braves were known as the Boston Red Stockings when the team was established in 1871. After three more name changes – Beaneaters, Doves and Rustlers, Boston's National League franchise settled for the Braves in 1912.

Two years later, the Braves finished with a miraculous season. They started the 1914 season by losing 18 of their first 22 games. By the Fourth of July, the Braves were in last place at 26-40, 15 games behind the New York Giants. Then, Boston got hot, winning 41 of its next 53 games in a span of two months.

After going 25-6 through September and October, the Braves won the National League pennant and earned a trip to the World Series to face the Philadelphia Athletics, who came out on top in three of the last four years. But in 1914, the Braves came out on top by pulling off a surprising four-game sweep over the A's.

The Braves played the World Series at Fenway Park since their home field, South End Grounds, was too small to play. The Miracle Braves celebrated their first world championship by beating the A's 3-1 in the fourth game, thanks to a two-out, two-run single by Johnny Evers in the bottom of the fifth.

Deal was also a valuable player in the game. He made the final out of the Series after fielding a grounder at third.

Born in Wilkinsburg, Pennsylvania, Deal was three weeks shy from his 23rd birthday when the Braves won it all. He joined the Boston franchise in 1913 after playing with the Tigers for the last year and a half. In 1914, Deal finished with 54 hits after getting 54 hits *combined* in the last three seasons. During his 10-year career with the Tigers, Braves, St. Louis Terriers (a Federal League team), St. Louis Browns and the Cubs, Deal finished with 752 hits. On the field, Deal played 823 out of his 851 games at the hot corner. He also led the National League third baseman in fielding three years in a row.

In the 1914 World Series, Deal struggled at the plate, getting just two hits – both were doubles – out of 16 at-bats. But he shined on the field, making no errors and six putouts, including the one with two outs in the top of the ninth in game four that was the most memorable of them all.

***

The Braves moved to Milwaukee in 1953. Four years later, they were world champions. The Braves earned a 4 games-to-3 victory over the Yankees by winning the seventh game of the 1957 World Series, 5-0 at Yankee Stadium.

The Yankees were threatening in the bottom of the ninth, having the bases loaded with two outs. But Bill Skowron grounded to Mathews at third, then Mathews stepped on third base to force out Jerry Coleman to end the game and the Series.

The final out of the 1957 World Series was one of many highlights in Mathews' career. Mathews made the out just three days shy from his 26th birthday. He was 20 years old when he made his major league debut with the Braves on April 15, 1952, when the team was playing in Boston.

The Boston Braves lost 89 games in the 1952 season, four years after winning the National League pennant. The next year, the Braves moved to Milwaukee, and won 92 games and finished second in the National League in their first season in Wisconsin. After finishing second by just one game behind Brooklyn in the 1956 season, the Braves came out on top in the NL in 1957, getting 95 victories and winning the league by eight games.

Photo by Baseball Digest; http://en.wikipedia.org/wiki/ File:Edwin_Lee_Mathews_ head_shot,_circa_1963.jpg

Mathews, who was born in Texarkana, Texas on Oct. 13, 1931, but later moved to Santa Barbara, California when he was a young boy, was a home run threat when he first stepped into the big leagues. He hit 25 home runs – including three in one game -- in 1952. He was over the 200 home run mark for his career after finishing with 32 dingers in 1957. After retiring in 1968 with the World Champion Detroit Tigers, Mathews finished with 512 career home runs.

Mathews went on to manage the Atlanta Braves from 1972 to 1974. He was the manager when Hank Aaron hit his 714th home run that broke Babe Ruth's mark on April 8, 1974. Mathews was inducted into the Hall of Fame in 1978.

Mathews died on Feb. 18, 2001, the same day legendary race car driver Dale Earnhardt perished in a crash at the Daytona 500.

***

Robinson was another Hall of Fame third baseman, earning a trip to Cooperstown in 1983. He played all of his 22 years in the majors with the Orioles and finished with 268 home runs, 1,357 RBIs and a .267 batting average, won 16 Gold Gloves and went to the All-Star game 18 times.

He also won a pair of World Series in 1966 and 1970, but it was 1970 that was the most memorable for Robinson. He helped the Orioles erase the sting from the five-game World Series loss to the Mets in 1969 by turning in one of the best defensive performances in World Series history in 1970.

Photo by Baltimore Orioles;
http://commons.wikimedia.
*org/wiki/File:Brooks_*
Robinson_1955.jpg

In game one, he made a spectacular backhanded grab of a grounder hit down the third base line by Lee May and spun to throw him out. In game three, Robinson saved a run in the top of the first by making a leaping grab of Tony Perez's hopper, stepping on third to force out Pete Rose and firing to first for the double play. In the second, he robbed a slow grounder hit by Tommy Helms and threw him out. In the sixth, Robinson made a diving catch of Johnny Bench's line drive.

Finally, the 33-year-old Robinson recorded the last out of the Series, fielding Pat Corrales' grounder and throwing him out to clinch the Orioles' second world title. Robinson earned MVP honors for his efforts at third base and at the plate. He hit .429 with two home runs and six RBIs in the five-game series against the Reds.

Robinson played all 22 years in the majors with the Orioles. After finishing his career in 1977, Robinson won 16 Gold Gloves, hit 267 with 268 home runs and 1,357 RBIs and 2,848 hits. In the 1970 season, he hit .276 with 18 home runs and 94 RBIs and helped the Orioles win 108 games, one win shy from their team record mark of 109 in 1969.

Before he shined in Baltimore, Robinson was shining in Little Rock, Arkansas. After graduating from Little Rock High School in 1955, Robinson was scouted for the University of Arkansas baseball program, then he played ball at South America and Cuba.

Robinson was drafted by the Orioles as an amateur free agent in 1955, a year after the Orioles moved to Baltimore. Nine years later, Robinson turned in his best offensive season, hitting .317 with 28 home runs and a league-leading 118 RBIs to win American League MVP honors.

Then, Robinson helped Baltimore become one of the powerhouses in the late 1960s-early 1970s as the Orioles won titles in 1966 and 1970 and American League championships in 1969 and 1971.

***

Another Hall of Fame third baseman made the final out of the 1911 World Series -- Home Run Baker.

In game six against the New York Giants at Shibe Park in Philadelphia, Baker became the first third baseman to make the final out of the World Series, fielding a ground ball hit by Art Wilson and throwing him out. The A's beat the Giants 13-2 in the sixth game to win the Series 4 games to 2 and their second straight world championship.

Baker also helped the A's win it all in 1910 and 1913. He joined the Philadelphia team in 1908 and later became part of the $100,000 infield that included Jack Barry, Eddie Collins and Stuffy McInnis.

Before he joined the A's, John Franklin Baker grew up in Maryland's Eastern Shore. He was born on March 13, 1886 in Trappe, a town of over 1,000 people. Baker died there on June 28, 1963 at age 77.

After playing in just nine games in 1908, Baker started becoming a hitting machine in 1909, leading the American League in triples with 19. Then, he became a home run threat in 1911, winning the first of four consecutive home run crowns with 11.

Baker hit two out of the park in the 1911 World Series, and that helped Baker earn his nickname, "Home Run." He hit the go-ahead home run in Philadelphia's 3-1 win in game two and a ninth-inning, game-tying home run in game three, which the A's won 3-2. Between 1911-1914, Baker hit a combined 42 home runs.

Baker helped the A's win 101 games and capture the American League pennant by 13.5 games over Detroit. He hit .334 with 115 RBIs and 40 doubles.

In the World Series, the 25-year-old Baker hit a team-high .375 with nine hits, seven runs scored and five RBIs. He batted .409 in 1910 and .450 in 1913.

Baker played another World Series for the A's in 1914, but his team lost to the Braves. He sat out the 1915 season due to a contract dispute.

Baker went to the Yankees in 1916 and played for four seasons before retiring in 1920. He returned to the Yankees in 1921 and helped them win back-to-back American League pennants before retiring again.

Baker was inducted to the Hall of Fame in 1955. He finished .307 with 96 home runs and 987 RBIs. In his seven seasons with the A's, he hit .321 with 48 home runs and 612 RBIs. He also never played a single inning in any position other than third base during his 13-year career.

***

During their time in New York, the Giants won five World Series championships. Their last world title came in 1954, when they swept the Cleveland Indians.

A piece of history was made with two outs and a runner on base in game four of that series in Cleveland Stadium, and the Giants were leading 7-4. Giants third baseman Hank Thompson caught a pop fly hit in foul territory by pinch hitter Dale Mitchell for the last out, making him the first African-American player to make the final out of the World Series.

Photo by Bowman Gum; http://commons. wikimedia.org/wiki/ File:Hank_Thompson_ Met_Museum_card.jpg

Just seven years before, Thompson was the first black player to play for the St. Louis Browns. He made his major league debut on July 17, 1947, three months after Jackie Robinson broke the color barrier.

When he joined the Giants in 1949, Thompson became the first black player to play in both the American and National Leagues. He, along with Monte Irvin, were the first black players to play for the Giants.

Thompson played in the World Series for the first time in 1951, but his team lost to the Yankees. Three years later, he won his first World Series championship after the Giants swept Cleveland.

New York qualified for the World Series by winning 97 games and the National League championship by five games over Brooklyn. The Giants beat a Cleveland team that won 111 games.

The final out by Thompson was overshadowed by Willie Mays' famous over-the-shoulder catch in game one at the Polo Grounds. Vic Wertz hit a 440-foot shot to center field, but Mays robbed it, keeping the game tied at 2-2. The Giants went on to win 5-2.

The 28-year-old Thompson hit .364 in the four games with a four-game World Series record seven walks. In game four, he walked three times, got a hit and an RBI and scored two runs.

Thompson stayed with the Giants until 1956. Two years later, the Giants moved west to San Francisco. They didn't celebrate another World Series title until 2010. The Giants won another championship in 2012.

Thompson was born on December 8, 1925 in Oklahoma City. At age 17, he started his professional baseball career with the Kansas City Monarchs of the Negro Baseball League. He also played with the Monarchs from 1946-1948.

Thompson died on September 30, 1969 at age 43 in Fresno, California.

***

For the first time since they were the Washington Senators in 1924, the Minnesota Twins were World Series champions in 1987.

In game seven of the Fall Classic against the Cardinals, Gary Gaetti ended the long championship drought by fielding a ground ball hit by St. Louis center fielder Willie McGee and threw him out for the final out.

Gaetti led all American League third basemen with 134 putouts in 1987. But on that October night in front of a large crowd with the Homer Hankies waving around at the Metrodome, Gaetti made his biggest putout of the season – and his major league baseball career.

Gaetti played for six teams for 19 years and celebrated his only World Series championship in 1987. He joined the Twins in 1981, when they were playing their final year at the Metropolitan Stadium. The next year, the Twins moved to the Metrodome. But changing stadiums didn't help the Twins – they lost 102 games and drew under a million fans.

When they won it all in 1987, the Twins drew over two million fans for the first time since they moved to the Twin Cities in 1961.

The Minnesota Twins were born in 1894 as the Kansas City Blues of the Western League. Seven years later, the Blues became the Washington Senators.

The Senators didn't celebrate their first winning season until 1912. They won their first World Series championship in 1924 after beating the New York Giants in seven games. Washington lost to the Pirates in seven games the next year and to the Giants in five games in 1933.

After 1933, the Senators hit a drought, finishing with just four winning seasons in the next 27 years. In 1961, the Senators became the Minnesota Twins. A new Washington Senators team was formed that year, but a decade later, the team moved to Dallas-Fort Worth to become the Texas Rangers.

In 1965, the Twins won their first American League pennant in 32 years, but lost to the Dodgers in seven games in the World Series. The Twins also won AL West Division titles in 1969 and 1970, but lost to the Orioles in the ALCS both years.

Then, the Twins hit another drought, finishing over .500 three times during the next 16 years. In 1987, Minnesota got brand new uniforms and got back on the winning track, winning 85 games and capturing its first division title in 17 years. The Twins advanced to the World Series by beating Detroit in five games in the ALCS.

Gaetti was a home run threat since he joined the Twins in September 1981. He hit a home run in his first major league at-bat. In his first full season in 1982, Gaetti hit 25 home runs. In the 1987 championship season, Gaetti hit 31 home runs and drove in 109 runs, making it the second year in a row he finished over 30 home runs and 100 RBIs. By 1987, he hit 138 career home runs.

The Twins were still playing in D.C. when Gaetti was born in Centralia, Illinois on August 19, 1958. Located 75 miles east of St. Louis, Centralia has the winningest high school boys basketball team in the country with over 2,124 wins and its nickname is the Orphans, originated in the early 1900s when the basketball team was playing in the state tournament, and the announcer commented that the squad looked like a bunch of orphans on the court after wearing non-matching red uniforms.

Gaetti was drafted by the Cardinals in the fourth round of the 1978 MLB Draft. Then, he was picked by the White Sox in the third round of the June secondary draft. Chicago is 280 miles north of Centralia.

But Gaetti wouldn't be playing in his home state or playing with a team just 75 miles away. He was picked by the Twins in the June secondary draft in 1979, so he would be playing over 600 miles away from home.

Gaetti played third base since he joined the Twins. He became a defensive standout, winning four straight Gold Glove awards, including one in 1987. He made just 11 errors at the hot corner that year.

The 29-year-old Gaetti made no errors at third base in the 1987 World Series, which the home team won all of its games. Trailing 3 games to 2, the Twins won 11-5 in game six and 4-2 in game seven.

Gaetti didn't make another World Series appearance. He stayed with the Twins until 1990. Gaetti also played with the Angels (1991-1993), Royals (1993-1995), Cardinals (1996-1998), Cubs (1998-1999) and Red Sox (2000).

Today, Gaetti is the manager of the Sugar Land Skeeters, an independent baseball team from the Atlantic League of Professional Baseball that plays in Sugar Land, Texas, a Houston suburb. In 2013, he earned the league's Manager of the Year honors after guiding the Skeeters to an all-time league-best 95 wins.

CHAPTER SIX: SHORTSTOP

Everett Scott and Cal Ripken, Jr. have three things in common.

They're shortstops, they played in more than 1,000 consecutive games and they made the last out of the World Series.

Scott became the first player to make the final out of the World Series twice in 1915 and 1916. Lou Gehrig, who later surpassed Scott's consecutive game streak, became the second player to accomplish that feat in 1936 and 1937.

Scott grew up in Bluffton, Indiana, a small town 30 miles south of Fort Wayne. Bluffton was founded in 1838 and was incorporated as a city in 1851, when it had 850 people.

Scott was born in Bluffton in 1892. He played baseball at Bluffton High before graduating in 1909. After playing pro ball at Kokomo, Ind., Fairmont, W.V. and Youngstown, Ohio, Scott got an offer to play for the Red Sox in 1913.

The next year, Scott joined the Red Sox after playing for their minor league team in St. Paul, Minn. In 1914, Scott hit .239 in 144 games. His Red Sox came up short of a bid for the World Series as they finished with 91 wins and eight games behind the Philadelphia A's, who lost to the Red Sox's city rivals, the Braves, in the World Series.

The next year, Boston beat Philadelphia in the World Series again. This time, it was the Red Sox who came out on top as they beat the Phillies in five games in the World Series. The Red Sox won 101 games to win their fourth

American League pennant and their first since 1912, when they beat the New York Giants on a walk-off sacrifice fly in game eight of the best of nine World Series.

The 22-year-old Scott got the final out of the World Series by fielding Bill Killefer's grounder and threw him out with no runners on base. The Red Sox beat the Phillies 5-4 in the fifth game at Baker Bowl in Philadelphia on a Harry Hooper solo home run in the top of the ninth.

The next year, Scott helped the Red Sox win another American League pennant. Boston finished with 91 wins and edged out the White Sox by two games in the league standings to advance to the World Series.

After batting a career-low .201 the year before, Scott finished .232 in 1916. But he turned in an outstanding defensive season, finishing with a .967 fielding percentage after making just 19 errors. He began a streak of seven straight years in leading American League shortstops in fielding percentage.

Scott also began his consecutive games played streak in 1916. In a span of nine years, the Deacon played in 1,307 straight games. And, to top it off, Scott picked up another World Series ring.

The Red Sox beat the Brooklyn Robins (now Dodgers) in five games to win their second straight crown and their third in five seasons. Boston beat Brooklyn 4-1 in game five at Fenway Park, and once again, Scott made the final out.

With two outs and a runner on base in the top of the ninth, Scott caught a pop fly hit by Mike Mowrey to end the game and the Series, making him the first player to make the final out of the Fall Classic twice.

Scott helped the Red Sox win again in 1918, but he didn't make the final out. His career at Boston continued until 1921. In 2008, Scott was posthumously inducted into the Red Sox Hall of Fame, 48 years after he died.

Scott joined the Red Sox's hated rivals, the Yankees, in 1922 and became the team's captain. The next year, Scott celebrated another World Series championship as the Yankees won the first of their 27 Fall Classic titles.

Scott's consecutive game played streak ended at 1,307 games on May 6, 1925. The next month, Scott was sent to the Washington Senators. After splitting the 1926 season with the White Sox and Reds, Scott retired.

Gehrig started his consecutive games played streak the same year Scott's streak ended. Gehrig broke Scott's record in 1933 in a game against the St. Louis Browns. He played in 2,130 straight games.

Then came Ripken.

Photo by Ronald Reagan Presidential Library & Museum/White House; http://commons.wikimedia. org/wiki/File:Ronald_Reagan_ with_Cal_Ripken_Jr.jpg

Ripken broke Gehrig's streak in a game against the Angels on Sept. 6, 1995. He played in 2,632 straight games before retiring in 2001.

He played in the All-Star Game 19 times, won two Gold Gloves, two American League MVPs and two All-Star Game MVPs, and won a World Series title with the Orioles in his first and only trip to the Fall Classic in 1983.

Ripken got the final out in the 1983 World Series against the Phillies, catching a line drive hit by Garry Maddox in game five at Veterans Stadium. Thanks to a pair of home runs by Eddie Murray, Baltimore beat Philadelphia 5-0 to win the Series four games to one.

The final out capped a tremendous 1983 season for Ripken, who joined the Orioles in 1981. He also earned his first of two American League MVP awards after hitting .318 with 27 home runs and 102 RBI and leading the league in doubles (47), hits (211) and runs scored (121).

Before he became a world champion baseball player in Baltimore, Ripken was growing up in Aberdeen, which is 36 miles northeast of Baltimore. Ripken grew up in a baseball family as his father, Cal, Sr., was a long-time baseball coach who managed the Orioles in the late 1980s and his brother, Billy, played baseball with Cal, Jr., at Aberdeen High and the Orioles.

Ripken was drafted by the Orioles in the second round of the 1978 MLB Draft. Three years later, he made his major league debut. In 1982, Ripken started his consecutive games-played streak and won American League Rookie of the Year honors after belting 28 home runs.

Ripken also came close to playing in the postseason in 1982. The Orioles won 94 games and finished one game behind the Brewers in the AL East Division after losing to Milwaukee on the last day of the season at Memorial Stadium.

The next year, Ripken got a chance to play in his first postseason after his Orioles finished with 98 victories and won the AL East by six games. Baltimore defeated the Chicago White Sox in the ALCS and knocked off the Phillies in the World Series for its third world championship.

With no runners on with two outs in the bottom of the ninth in game five of the Fall Classic, Maddox lined an 0-2 pitch to the 23-year-old Ripken to end the contest and the Series. With that, Ripken joined Brooks Robinson and Paul Blair as the only Baltimore players to make the final out of the World Series.

After making the final out of the 1983 World Series, Ripken would never play in another World Series game. He played in the postseason two more times before retiring in 2001. The Orioles played in the ALCS in 1996 and 1997, but lost both times to the Yankees and Indians, respectively.

Scott and Ripken are two of 14 shortstops who recorded the final out of the World Series. The first shortstop to get the final out of the World Series was the New York Giants' Bill Dahlen in 1905.

***

After boycotting the 1904 World Series, the New York Giants were back in the Fall Classic in 1905.

And they brought home the National League's first world championship after beating the Philadelphia A's 4 games to 1. Two years before, the Boston Americans (now the Red Sox) beat the Pittsburgh Pirates in the first World Series.

Boston pitcher Bill Dinneen recorded the last out in the 1903 World Series. Another Bill got the last out in the 1905 World Series, this time his name was Bill Dahlen.

Dahlen fielded a ground ball hit by Lave Cross and threw him out to clinch the Giants' first of their seven world titles. New York beat Philadelphia 2-0 at the Polo Grounds behind a complete-game shutout by Christy Mathewson, and it was Dahlen's last World Series game.

Dahlen was born on January 5, 1870 in Nelliston, New York, a village in Montgomery County which is an hour drive west of Albany.

The New York Giants didn't exist when Dahlen was born. They were established in 1883 as the New York Gothams. In 1885, they became the New York Giants after manager Jim Mutrie stormed into the dressing room and shouted "My big fellows! My giants!" after his team got a big victory over the Phillies.

Dahlen started his baseball career in 1891 with the Chicago Colts (now Cubs) and stayed with them until 1898. He was traded to the Brooklyn Superbas and helped them win National League titles in 1899 and 1900.

In 1904, Dahlen joined the Giants. He led the National League in RBIs with 80. But Dahlen didn't get a chance to play in his first World Series after the Giants refused to play in the Fall Classic against the Red Sox because they thought the American League was a minor league.

The next year, Dahlen got to play in his first World Series after the Giants won 105 games and the National League pennant by nine games. Dahlen hit .242 with seven home runs and 81 RBIs in the regular season. In the World Series, the 35-year-old Dahlen had no hits out of 15 at-bats with a run scored and an RBI, but made no errors at shortstop.

After four seasons with the Giants, Dahlen joined the Boston Doves (now the Atlanta Braves) in 1908. He returned to Brooklyn in 1910 and retired as a player after the 1911 season. Dahlen was Brooklyn's player-manager from 1910-1913.

During his managerial career, Dahlen had a ferocious temper when arguing, drawing 65 ejections and giving him the nickname "Bad Bill."

Dahlen died in Brooklyn at age 80 on December 5, 1950. At the end of his career, he held the major league record for career games played (2,443), ranked second in walks (1,064) and fifth in at bats (9,033), and was among the top 10 in RBIs (1,234), doubles (414) and extra base hits (661).

***

In 1907, Joe Tinker clinched the Cubs' first World Series title by catching a pop fly hit by the Detroit Tigers' Boss Schmidt in game five, which the Cubs won 2-0. Chicago won the best-of-nine series, 4 games to none with a tie.

Before they were known as the Lovable Losers, the Cubs were big time winners on the field, winning back-to-back World Series titles in 1907 and 1908. They were first known as the Chicago White Stockings when the team was founded in 1870. They didn't play in 1872 and 1873 because of the after effects from the Great Chicago Fire. In 1876, the White Stockings won the first ever National League pennant.

Then, the White Stockings became the Colts in 1890 and Orphans in 1898 before they stuck with the Cubs in 1902.

Tinker also started his major league career with the Cubs in 1902. He won the Cubs' starting shortstop job that year. After making 72 errors at shortstop in his rookie season, Tinker quickly blossomed into a solid shortstop, leading in the National League in double plays turned in 1905 and finished with a .944 fielding percentage in 1906.

Tinker started playing baseball while growing up in Kansas. Born in 1880, Tinker played baseball for his school's team in Kansas City, Kansas, when he was 14.

Tinker also played semi-professional baseball in Kansas towns such as Parsons and Coffeyville. After playing with minor league teams such as the Denver Grizzlies, Great Falls (Montana) Indians and Helena (Montana) Senators and the Portland (Ore.) Webfoots, Tinker joined the Cubs, and he later became part of a great double play combination with teammates Johnny Evers and Frank Chance that was immortalized as "Tinker-to-Evers-to-Chance" in the poem, "Baseball Sad Lexicon."

Tinker helped the Cubs win 116 games, a record for victories that was broken by the Mariners in 1999. But the Cubs lost to the White Sox in six games in the World Series.

The next year, Tinker was a World Series champion. He helped the Cubs win 107 games and knock off the Tigers in five games in the Fall Classic.

In game five at Bennett Park in Detroit, the Cubs scored a run in the first and another in the second. The Tigers were threatening in the bottom of the ninth after Claude Rossman singled to right with one out. With two outs, Schmidt came in to pinch hit for Jimmy Archer. Schmidt flied out to the 27-year-old Tinker for the final out of the game, the Series and the 1907 season.

Tinker had one of his worst hitting seasons of his career in 1907, batting .221. But he shined on the field, finishing with a .939 fielding percentage at shortstop.

Tinker helped the Cubs win another World Series in 1908. He played in his fourth World Series in 1910, but his Cubs lost to the Philadelphia A's. After playing 10 years with the Cubs, Tinker played one season with the Reds in 1913. He also played two seasons with the Chicago Whales of the Federal League before returning to the Cubs in 1916 as their player-manager.

Tinker finished his career with a .262 batting average with 31 home runs, 782 RBIs and 336 stolen bases. He was inducted to the Baseball Hall of Fame in 1946, two years before he died on his 68th birthday in Orlando, Florida.

***

Another shortstop named Joe helped the Cleveland Indians win their first world title in 1920 by getting the final out of the Fall Classic against the Brooklyn Robins.

The world championship became a late birthday present for Joe Sewell. The Indians won it all just three days after Sewell's 22nd birthday on Oct. 12.

Long before he was celebrating a world championship in the Midwest, Sewell was growing up in the South. He was born on Oct. 9, 1898 in Titus, Alabama, which is 75 miles south of Birmingham. Sewell graduated from Wetumpka High in 1916, and he lettered in college football for the University of Alabama from 1917-1919. Sewell-Thomas Stadium, Alabama's baseball stadium, is named in Sewell's honor and fans nickname it "The Joe."

By the time Sewell was born in Alabama, the Cleveland Indians were playing baseball in Michigan as the Grand Rapids Rustlers of the Western League. They were established in 1894. The next year, they moved to Cleveland and became the Cleveland Lake Shores. Then, they were the Bluebirds, then the Broncos and the Naps. In 1915, the nickname was changed to the Indians.

After finishing second in the American League the last two years, the Indians came out on top in 1920, winning 98 games. But on August 17, tragedy struck the Indians.

Shortstop Ray Chapman died of injuries from a pitched ball in a game against the Yankees the day before.

Sewell took over shortstop duties and became valuable, hitting .329 with 23 hits and 12 RBIs in 22 games played. He made his major league debut on Sept. 10.

The Indians beat Brooklyn 5 games to 2 in the best of the nine series. Sewell played in all seven games against Brooklyn and got just four hits. But his biggest highlight was getting the final out in game seven at Dunn Field in Cleveland.

With the Indians leading 3-0 with Brooklyn having a runner on first and two outs, Ed Konetchy hit a grounder to Sewell. Sewell threw the ball to second baseman Bill Wambsganss to force out Hi Myers at second for the final out.

Sewell was on his way to a Hall of Fame career. He hit .318 with 101 runs scored, 93 RBI and a .412 on-base percentage in 1921. Sewell played 12 seasons with the Indians before heading to New York in 1931 to play for the Yankees. He helped the Yankees win it all in 1932.

After retiring in 1933, Sewell finished with 2,226 hits, 1,055 RBIs and a .312 batting average. He also holds the record for the lowest strikeout rate in major league history, striking out on average only once every 63 at-bats, and the most consecutive games without a strikeout. His 167.7 at-bats per strikeout in 1932 remains a single-season record. The efforts earned Sewell a trip to Cooperstown in 1977. Sewell died in Mobile, Alabama in 1990.

***

Pee Wee Reese was another shortstop from the South who made the final out of the World Series. He recorded the last out in the 1955 Fall Classic, where the Brooklyn Dodgers finally picked up their first championship, beating the Yankees in seven games.

Harold Peter Henry Reese was born on July 23, 1918, two years after the Dodgers won their first National League pennant. During that time, the Dodgers were known as the Brooklyn Robins.

When Brooklyn established a baseball team in 1883, it went through a variety of nicknames – the Bridegrooms, Grooms, Superbas, Robins and Trolley Dodgers. The team began as the Brooklyn Atlantics.

Harold Reese had a pair of nicknames, Pee Wee and the Little Colonel. But he was well known as Pee Wee. He got that nickname because he was a standout marbles player while growing up in Kentucky. Reese was born in Ekron, a town 50 miles southwest of Louisville. At age eight, he moved to Louisville.

Reese didn't start playing baseball until his senior year at duPoint Manual High School. He began his major league career in 1940 with the Brooklyn Dodgers.

Brooklyn officially adopted the Dodgers nickname in 1932. By the time Reese joined the team, the Dodgers had won a pair of National League pennants in 1916 and 1920, but lost in the World Series both years. Coincidentally, their seasons ended with a groundout to a shortstop.

The Dodgers won National League pennants in 1941, 1947, 1949, 1952 and 1953, but didn't win the big one in either of those years. By 1953, Reese established himself as a standout shortstop, making nine All-Star Game appearances.

Reese finally got his first World Series championship in his sixth try on Oct. 4, 1955, when the Dodgers beat the Yankees 2-0 in game seven at Yankee Stadium.

With no runners on base and two outs in the bottom of the ninth, the 37-year-old Reese fielded a grounder hit by Elston Howard and threw him out to clinch the Dodgers' first title.

Reese and the Dodgers went back to the World Series the next year, but lost to the Yankees in seven games. Reese played two more years before retiring in 1958, when the Dodgers played their first season in Los Angeles.

Reese hit .269 with 126 home runs and 885 RBIs. In the 1955 season, he hit .282 after hitting over .300 for the first and only time of his career the year before. Reese played in the All-Star Game 10 times, including nine straight from 1946-1954, and was inducted to the Baseball Hall of Fame in 1984.

Reese died on Aug. 14, 1999 at age 81 in Louisville.

***

In 1963, the Dodgers won their second world title in Los Angeles by sweeping the Yankees in four games. Maury Wills, who stole 586 bases during his career, stole the Yankees' hopes of winning their third straight title by making the final out in game four. The Yankees had runners on first and second with two outs when Hector Lopez grounded out to Wills for the final out of the game and the Series.

Wills was born on Oct. 2, 1932 in Washington, D.C. A month later, Franklin Delano Roosevelt showed the United States that happy days are here again as he defeated Herbert Hoover in the election for President of the United States.

Wills attended Cardozo Senior High in northwest Washington. Other famous alumni included J. Edgar Hoover and Marvin Gaye. While at Cardozo, Wills earned All-City honors in football, basketball and baseball.

Wills joined the Dodgers in 1959, the same year they won the World Series. Wills played in just 83 games.

Then, Willis became a stolen base threat, leading the National League in stolen bases six straight years. In 1962, he stole 104 bases to set a new Major League record. He earned All-Star Game and National League Most Valuable Player honors that same year.

In 1963, Wills added another World Series ring to go with that hardware he won in 1962. The Dodgers clinched their third World Series title with a 2-1 win over the Yankees at Dodger Stadium. Los Angeles defeated New York 5-2 in game one on Wills' 31st birthday.

Wills stole just 40 bases in 1963, but they were good enough to win the National League stolen base title for the fourth straight year. He also hit a career best .302, which he later tied in 1967 while playing with the Pirates.

In 1962, the Dodgers finished second to the San Francisco Giants with a 102-63 record after losing to the Giants 2 games to 1 in a best-of three game playoff to decide the National League pennant. In 1963, the Dodgers advanced to the World Series by winning 99 games and the NL pennant by six games over the Cardinals.

Wills would play in two more World Series in 1965 and 1966 with the Dodgers. Los Angeles beat Minnesota in 1965, but lost to Baltimore in 1966.

In 1967, Wills was sent to the Pirates and played for them for two seasons. After starting the 1969 season with the expansion Montreal Expos, Wills headed back to L.A. and played for the Dodgers until 1972.

***

Leo Durocher coached, managed and played for the Brooklyn/Los Angeles Dodgers. He won 2,008 games as a manager of the Dodgers, New York Giants, Cubs and Astros.

Before he joined the Dodgers organization, Durocher was a member of "The Gashouse Gang" at St. Louis, helping the Cardinals win their third World Series title in 1934. Durocher joined the Cardinals in 1933 and played in St. Louis for five seasons before heading to the Dodgers in 1938.

The captain and shortstop of the Cardinals, Durocher made the final out in game seven of the 1934 World Series against Detroit. With the Tigers having runners on first and second, Durocher fielded a grounder hit by Marv Owen, then threw the ball to second baseman Frankie Frisch to force out Billy Rogell at second to end the Series.

But the game ended even before the final out was recorded – the Cardinals scored seven runs in the third en route to an 11-0 win over the Tigers to win the series four games to three.

Durocher won his second World Series title in 1934. He helped the Yankees win it all in 1928, when they swept the Cardinals in four games.

Durocher, who was born on July 27, 1905 in West Springfield, Massachusetts, began his major league career with the Yankees in 1925 and

Photo by Goudey Gum Company; http://commons. wikimedia.org/wiki/ File:LeoDurocherGoudeycard.jpg

played just two games. After a two-year hiatus, Durocher returned to the Yankees and helped them win their third world title.

Durocher headed to the Reds in 1930 and stayed with them until mid-season 1933, when he was traded to the Cardinals.

In 1934, Durocher played a career-high 146 games, and hit .260 with three homers and 70 RBIs. His Cardinals won 95 games, edged the New York Giants by two games for the National League pennant and came back from a 3 games to 2 deficit to win the World Series.

The 29-year-old Durocher had seven hits with four runs scored in the World Series. He had two hits and a run scored in the seventh game, which was his final World Series game as a player.

Durocher played with the Dodgers from 1938-1941, 1943 and 1945. He became the team's manager from 1939-1946 and 1948.

Durocher managed the Giants from 1948-1955 and won a World Series title in 1954. He became the Cubs' manager in 1966 and stayed there until midseason 1972. He managed the Astros for the final 31 games in 1972 and the entire 1973 season before retiring.

Durocher died on October 7, 1991 in Palm Springs, California. He was posthumously inducted to Cooperstown three years later.

***

In 1935, the Tigers won their first World Series championship, beating the Cubs in six games. In 1945, they won again and they beat the Cubs again, this time in seven games.

Skeeter Webb, who hit just .199 during the regular season, fielded the final out in game seven of the Fall Classic at Wrigley Field. To date, it was the last time the Cubs played a World Series game.

James Laverne Webb was born in Meridian, Mississippi in 1909, the same year the Tigers lost in the World Series for the third year in a row. Webb attended Ole Miss before starting his major league career in 1932 with the Cardinals. He played in just one game with the Redbirds.

Webb didn't make another major league team until 1938, when he joined the Indians. In 1940, Webb was traded to the White Sox and played with the South Siders for five seasons.

In 1945, Webb joined the Tigers, and he got to be part of a league championship team for the first time. He helped Detroit win 88 games and the American League pennant by one game over the Washington Senators. It was Detroit's seventh American League pennant.

The Tigers were established in 1894. They won their first American League pennant in 1907, but lost to the Cubs in the World Series. Detroit lost to the Cubs in the World Series again in 1908 and to Pittsburgh in 1909.

The Tigers went back to the World Series in 1934, but they lost to the Cardinals in seven. In 1935, Detroit won its first world crown by beating the Cubs in six games. The Series ended on a Goose Goslin walk-off single in the bottom of the ninth.

The Tigers won another AL pennant in 1940, but lost to the Reds in seven games.

With the Tigers winning the AL pennant in 1945, Webb got to play in the World Series for the first time. Despite hitting just .185, Webb will be best known for the making the final out of the World Series, and the Tigers didn't have to win the World Series on a walk-off hit.

With Chicago having a runner on first, the 35-year-old Webb fielded a grounder hit by Don Johnson. Webb threw the ball to second baseman Eddie Mayo to force out Roy Hughes at second to end the game. Webb also scored a pair of runs as Detroit beat the Cubs 9-3.

Webb remained with the Tigers until 1947. He played one last season with the Philadelphia A's. Webb died in 1986 in Meridian.

***

The Yankees had one shortstop who recorded the final out in the Fall Classic and he was Frankie Crosetti. Crosetti helped the Yankees win their eighth world title with a four-game sweep over the Reds in 1939.

New York beat Cincinnati 7-4 in 10 innings in the fourth game. The Reds were threatening in the bottom of the 10th, having runners on first and second. Wally Berger was at the plate, representing the tying run. But Berger lined out to Crosetti to clinch another Yankee championship.

The Yankees won the world title just four days after Crosetti's 29th birthday. It was Crosetti's fifth world championship, and he would add three World Series rings to his trophy case before retiring as a player in 1948. Crosetti also coached the Yankees for 22 years (1946-1968) and won nine more World Series rings.

Before he was dazzling at the East Coast, Crosetti was growing up at the West Coast. He was born on Oct. 4, 1910 in San Francisco, 27 years before the Golden Gate Bridge was built. He played four seasons with the San Francisco Seals of the Pacific Coast League before joining the Yankees in 1932.

Crosetti was part of a world championship team in his first year in the majors as the Yankees swept the Cubs in the World Series. They won game four just two days shy of Crosetti's 22nd birthday.

Known as the Crow, Crosetti turned in one of his best defensive seasons in 1939, leading American League shortstops in putouts (323) and double plays (118). He also led the league in at-bats with 656.

Crosetti and the Yankees won their fourth straight American League title after winning 106 games and the league by a whopping 17 games over Boston. Even though it took 10 innings to win the fourth game, the Yankees had an easy time with the Reds, outscoring them 20-8 in the four games.

After hitting .194 in 1940, Crosetti lost his shortstop job to Phil Rizzuto in 1941 but got it back when Rizzuto entered the military during World War II. When Rizzuto returned, Crosetti became a reserve player once again, and later the Yankees' third-base coach. He died in 2002 at age 91 in Stockton, California.

***

After playing in the American League the last six years, Jackie Hernandez switched to the National League in 1971.

This time, he was playing for the Pittsburgh Pirates. And his first season in the Steel City was one he'll never forget.

First, he helped the Pirates become the first major league team to field an all-black/minority lineup. Then, he made the final out of the 1971 World Series by fielding a ground ball that was hit by Baltimore's Merv Rettenmund and threw him out to clinch the Pirates' fourth world championship and their first since 1960, when Bill Mazeroski hit a walk-off, solo home run in the seventh game against the Yankees.

The Pirates beat the Orioles 2-1 in game seven at Memorial Stadium in Baltimore to win four games to three. Pittsburgh rallied from a 2 games to 0 deficit to deny Baltimore its second straight world championship.

Jacinto Zulueta Hernandez was born on Sept. 11, 1940 in Central Tinguaro, Cuba. He started his major league career with the California Angels in 1965. Then, he went to the Twins in 1967 and played for two seasons. Hernandez joined the expansion Kansas City Royals in 1969 and played there for two more years.

In 1971, Hernandez joined the Pirates and hit just .206 with three home runs and 26 RBIs in 88 games. On September 1, 1971 in a game against the Phillies at Three Rivers Stadium, Hernandez was part of an all-black/minority starting lineup that included Roberto Clemente, Willie Stargell, Manny Sanguillen, Dock Ellis, Rennie Stennett, Dave Cash, Al Oliver and Gene Clines. Pittsburgh won 10-7, while Hernandez had a run scored and an RBI.

The Pirates went on to win the NL East Division crown for the second straight year. They advanced to the World Series by knocking off San Francisco in four games in the NLCS.

In the World Series, Pittsburgh defeated a Baltimore club that won 101 games. After throwing out Rettenmund on a groundout for the final out, the 31-year-old Hernandez helped Steve Blass throw a four-hit complete game.

Hernandez played two more years with the Pirates before retiring in 1973.

***

The Oakland A's won another World Series championship in 1973. This time, they celebrated in front of their home fans.

After clinching the Fall Classic in Cincinnati in 1972, the A's won their second straight title in 1973 by beating the New York Mets 5-2 in the seventh game at Oakland-Alameda County Coliseum to win the Series 4 games to 3.

Shortstop Bert Campaneris was big at the plate and on the field in game seven. He hit a two-run homer in the bottom of the third that helped Oakland take a 2-0 lead. Then in the top of the ninth, he caught a pop fly hit by the Mets' Wayne Garrett to clinch the A's championship.

Campaneris was valuable for the A's ever since he started playing for them in 1964, when the team was playing in Kansas City. He holds the team's records for career games played, hits and at-bats. "Campy" played for the Kansas City/Oakland A's for 13 seasons, then, he played for the Rangers (1977-1979), Angels (1979-1981) and Yankees (1983).

Campaneris was born on March 9, 1942 in Pueblo Nuevo, Cuba. At age 22, Campaneris hit two home runs in his first game on July 23, 1964, becoming one of five players to accomplish that feat.

The next year, Campaneris won the first of his six stolen base titles. He also led the American League in triples.

When the A's moved to Oakland in 1968, Campaneris led the league in hits with 177.

In 1973, Campaneris had four home runs and 46 RBIs and 89 runs scored to help the A's win their third consecutive AL West Division title, their second straight American League pennant and their second consecutive world championship.

The A's won 94 games in the regular season. They advanced to the World Series against the Mets by beating Baltimore in five games in the ALCS.

The Mets, who won it all in 1969, had a 3 games to 2 lead before the A's won both game six and seven at Oakland. In the top of the ninth, the Mets had runners on first and third and Garrett represented the tying run at the plate. But after Garrett flied out to the 31-year-old Campaneris, the 1973 World Series ended the same way it started, with Garrett popping up to the infield.

Campaneris finished with nine hits, six runs scored and three RBIs in the World Series. The A's had no home runs in the Fall Classic until Campy hit one out in the bottom of the third in game seven. And he also became the first A's shortstop to record the final out of the World Series since Jack Barry in 1910.

***

Jack Barry helped the Philadelphia Athletics become a baseball powerhouse in the 1910s. The A's won World Series championships in 1910, 1911 and 1913. By 1913, Philadelphia became the first team to win three World Series championships.

Barry was part of the $100,000 infield that included second baseman Eddie Collins, third baseman Home Run Baker and first baseman Stuffy McInnis.

Before he started his major league career at the City of Brotherly Love, John Joseph Barry was a New Englander. He was born on April 26, 1887 in Meriden, Connecticut, and played college baseball at Holy Cross, located in Worcester, Massachusetts.

The Philadelphia A's were born in 1901 as one of the founding members of the American League and a city rival baseball team of the Phillies of the National League. They finished with a winning record every year until Barry joined the team in 1908. That year, the A's finished sixth out of eight teams at 68-85. Barry played in just 40 games.

Philadelphia got back of the winning track in 1909, finishing second in the American League and Barry's playing time began to increase. The next year, the A's, managed by Connie Mack, started their dynasty, winning their first American League pennant and finishing with 102 wins to advance to the World Series against the Cubs.

The A's beat the two-time champion Cubs four games to one. Philadelphia beat Chicago 7-2 in the fifth game at West Side Grounds in Chicago.

Barry was the A's everyday shortstop, but he led the American League in errors with 63. But the 23-year-old Barry made sure he didn't make an error with two outs in the bottom of the ninth. With Jimmy Archer at first, Johnny Kling – who recorded the final out in 1908 World Series -- grounded to Barry and Barry stepped on second to force out Archer for the final out to clinch the A's first World Series championship.

Barry had four hits with two doubles, three runs scored and three RBIs in the Series. During the regular season, he hit .259 with three homers and 60 RBIs.

Barry helped the A's win it all in 1911 and 1913. After Philadelphia was upset by the Boston Braves in the 1914 Fall Classic, Barry went back to New England, this time he was a member of the Boston Red Sox. He was moved to second base, and helped Boston win back-to-back championships in 1915 and 1916.

Barry became Boston's player-manager in 1917. He retired in 1919 with the Red Sox.

Barry coached the Holy Cross baseball team for 40 years until his death on April 23, 1961. His Holy Cross squad won the College World Series in 1952.

***

Photo by Keith Allison; http://commons.wikimedia.org/wiki/File:AAAA4973_Juan_Uribe.jpg

Juan Uribe was another shortstop who celebrated World Series championships for two different teams – the White Sox in 2005 and the Giants in 2010.

His first world championship in 2005 was memorable. He helped the White Sox win their first World Series championship in 88 years by getting the final two outs in game four, which was won by Chicago 1-0 over the Houston Astros.

Before he became a World Series champion, Uribe was growing up in the Dominican Republic. His second cousin, Jose, played in the World Series in 1989 with the Giants, but didn't win.

Juan Uribe started his major league career with the Colorado Rockies in 2001. He was traded to the White Sox in 2004. A year later, he was named Chicago's starting shortstop and he became one of the key players, finishing with 121 hits, 23 doubles, 16 home runs and 74 RBIs and helping the White Sox win 99 games, one win short from their franchise record of 100 wins that was set in 1917.

Since their last World Series title in 1917, the South Siders went through a long drought. In 1919, they were marred by the Black Sox Scandal, which the team was accused of throwing the World Series to the Reds, who won five games to three.

The White Sox didn't win another American League pennant until 1959, when they lost to the Dodgers in six games in the World Series. They won AL West Division titles in 1983, 1993 and 2000, but they didn't climb over that ALCS hurdle.

The White Sox climbed over that hurdle by beating the Angels in five games in the ALCS. The win over the Angels gave the Uribe a chance to play in the World Series, just like his second cousin.

Uribe's first trip to the World Series was memorable. The White Sox cruised to a four-game sweep over the Astros, who were making their first trip to the Fall Classic.

In game four at Minute Maid Park, Chicago scored its only run in the top of the eighth on an RBI single by World Series MVP Jermaine Dye.

The Astros were threatening in the bottom of the ninth. Jason Lane led off the inning with single. He moved to second on a sacrifice bunt by Brad Ausmus.

Then, the 26-year-old Uribe caught a ball hit by Chris Burke in foul territory and crashed into the third base stands for the second out. Finally, Uribe fielded a slow grounder hit by Orlando Palmeiro and threw him out for the final out of the Series.

Thanks to that last out by Uribe, all of Chicago, especially in the South Side, celebrated all night. White Sox fans have waited since 1917 to watch that last out of the World Series made by a White Sox player. October 26, 2005 was a night White Sox fans – and Uribe -- would never forget.

Uribe joined the Giants in 2009. The next year, he helped them win their first World Series title since they moved to San Francisco in 1958. He currently plays for the Dodgers.

CHAPTER SEVEN: LEFT FIELD

The Texas Rangers had not one, but two chances to get the final out of the 2011 World Series.

They blew both chances.

The Cardinals' Allen Craig made sure he wasn't going to blow a chance to get the final out of this memorable Fall Classic, won by the Cardinals four games to three. When the Cardinal left fielder caught a fly ball hit by David Murphy on the warning track in game seven at Busch Stadium, it capped a miraculous season by the Cardinals, who won 90 games, came back from a 10.5-game deficit in August to beat the Atlanta Braves for the final playoff spot in the National League, upset the Phillies in five games in the NLDS and beat the Brewers in six games in the NLCS to advance to the World Series against the Rangers.

In game six at Busch Stadium, the Cardinals were down to their last out in the bottom of the ninth when Series MVP David Freese hit a two-run double to tie the game at 7-7. Trailing 9-8 in the bottom of the 10th, St. Louis was down to its last out before Lance Berkman hit a game-tying RBI single. Then, Freese finished it up with a solo home run in the bottom of the 11th to give the Cardinals a 10-9 win.

In game seven, the 27-year-old Craig hit a go-ahead, game-winning solo home run in the third on a full count to break a 2-2 tie. He later robbed Nelson Cruz of a home run in the top of the sixth. Finally, Craig became the 12th left fielder to make the final out of the World Series. The

Cardinals won the seventh game 6-2 to win their 11th World Series title.

"The whole experience was awesome," Craig told the St. Louis Post-Dispatch on Oct. 30, 2011. "Hitting a home run was awesome and I've never robbed a home run like that. I was glad to do it in the seventh game of the World Series. It's all about making the best of your opportunities. You can't let opportunities slip."

Then, more good things started to pile up for Craig. He married his wife, Marie, two weeks after game seven of the 2011 World Series. Then, he celebrated Allen Craig Day on January 10, 2012 in his hometown of Temecula, Calif., named in his honor following the 2011 World Series win.

Craig was born on July 18, 1984 in Mission Viejo, California, located in Orange County. He played high school ball at Chaparral High School in Temecula, which is in Riverside County. Craig stayed in California for college ball as he played for the University of California at Berkeley. He played for the USA Junior National team in Canada in 2002.

Craig joined the Cardinals in 2010. The next year, he hit .315 with 11 home runs and 40 RBIs. He had five hits, three of them were homers, five runs scored and five RBIs in the World Series against the Rangers.

By catching Murphy's fly ball, Craig became the first left fielder to make the last out since the Yankees' Chad Curtis in 1999.

In 2013, Craig hit .315 with 13 home runs and 97 RBIs and played in the All-Star Game for the first time, but his season was cut short due to a foot injury in September. Craig helped the Cardinals return to the World Series in 2013, but they lost to the Red Sox in six games. Craig played in all six games and finished with six hits. He was well known for scoring the game-winning run on an obstruction call in the bottom of the ninth inning of game three at Busch Stadium that gave the Cardinals a 5-4 win.

***

When he caught Atlanta's Keith Lockhart's pop fly in game four of the 1999 Fall Classic at Yankee Stadium, Curtis helped the Yankees win their second straight title. New York beat Atlanta 4-1 in the fourth game to sweep the series and win its 25th world championship.

Curtis played for five different teams before joining the Yankees in 1997. He didn't play in the 1998 World Series, but he still received a ring. The next year, Curtis hit .262 in 99 games, but he still earned a spot on the postseason roster.

Born in Marion, Indiana on November 6, 1968, Curtis played in the World Series for the first time in his major league career. He started his career in 1992 with the California Angels. After three seasons in Anaheim, Curtis headed to the Tigers in 1995. He split the 1996 season with Detroit and the Dodgers. Curtis started the 1997 season with the Indians before being traded to the Yankees later that year.

In 1999, the Yankees won 98 games, captured the American League East Division by four games, swept the Rangers in the ALDS and knocked off the Red Sox in five games in the ALCS to advance to their third World Series in four years. New York outscored the Braves 23-9 in the four games in the World Series.

In the World Series against Atlanta, the 20-year-old Curtis hit a walk-off home run in game three and, in game four, became the fourth Yankee left fielder to make the final out of the World Series. The other Yankee left fielders were Babe Ruth, Gene Woodling and Hector Lopez.

Game four was the last contest in a Yankee uniform for Curtis. He played the next two seasons with the Rangers before retiring with 101 home runs and a .264 batting average.

***

Yes, it's true -- the Sultan of Swat made the final out of the 1928 World Series against the Cardinals. Two years before, Ruth was thrown out at second trying to steal and the out ended the seventh game and the Series and gave the Cardinals their first world title.

On Oct. 9, 1928, the 33-year-old Ruth made up for that by catching Frankie Frisch's pop fly in foul territory at Sportsman's Park with two runners on and two outs to give the Yankees their second straight world title and their third overall.

Ruth also hit three home runs in game four. New York won 7-3 to complete the four-game sweep over the St. Louis and helped Ruth redeem himself from that disappointing ending in the 1926 World Series.

During his 21-year career, Ruth played on seven World Series championship teams. He helped the Red Sox win three titles and the Yankees four.

Ruth was best known as the one of the greatest home run hitters of all-time, as he hit 714 home runs, a mark that was broken by Hank Aaron and Barry Bonds.

Before he became one of the greatest home run hitters of all time and a seven-time World Series champion, George Herman Ruth was growing up in Baltimore. He was born there on February 6, 1895. When he was seven, Ruth was sent to the St. Mary's Industrial School for Boys, which is an orphanage, and spent much of the next 12 years there.

After playing minor league baseball with the Baltimore Orioles, Ruth joined the Red Sox in 1914. He helped the Red Sox win World Series titles in 1915, 1916 and 1918. Ruth was a pitcher for the Red Sox, winning 89 games and capturing an American League ERA title in his six seasons in Boston.

After being sold to the Yankees in December 1919, Ruth converted to an everyday outfielder and big power hitter. And he also helped the Yankees become a World Series powerhouse.

Ruth celebrated his first World Series championship as a Yankee in 1923. That year, Yankee Stadium was opened and it was quickly nicknamed as "The House That Ruth Built." Ruth also helped the Yankees win again in 1927.

In 1928, the Yankees qualified for the World Series by winning the American League pennant by just three games over the Philadelphia A's. Ruth led the American League in homers (54) and RBIs (142).

In the World Series against the Cardinals, Ruth finished with the second-highest batting average in World Series history at .625. He had 10 hits, nine runs scored, three home runs and four RBIs.

Ruth won his final World Series championship in 1932, when the Yankees swept the Cubs in four games. He hit two home runs in game three, including his famous "Called Shot."

After playing two more seasons with the Yankees, Ruth wrapped up his baseball career in 1935 in the same city where it started – Boston. This time, he played with the Boston Braves.

Ruth was one of the first inductees in the Baseball Hall of Fame in 1936. He died in 1948 at New York City at age 53.

***

In the 1952 World Series against the Brooklyn Dodgers, Woodling became the first player to pinch hit a triple in the Fall Classic. He also made the final out by catching Pee Wee Reese's fly ball in left field with no runners on and two outs at Ebbets Field, giving the Yankees their fourth straight World Series title.

Photo by Bowman Gum; http://commons.wikimedia.org/wiki/File:Gene_Woodling_1953.jpg

Woodling played for the Yankees for six seasons (1949-1954) and helped New York win world titles in five of them (1949, 1950, 1951, 1952 and 1953). He also played for five other teams.

Woodling was born on Aug. 16, 1922 in Akron, Ohio. His major league baseball career began in Ohio in 1943, as he became a member of the Indians. After a two-year hiatus, Woodling returned to the Indians in 1946. He played one season with the Pirates in 1947. After not playing in the majors in 1948, Woodling joined the Yankees in 1949.

Woodling turned in one of his best hitting seasons in 1952, hitting .309 with 12 home runs and 63 runs batted in. He also led American League left fielders with a .996 fielding percentage and made just one error.

The Yankees advanced to the World Series by getting 95 victories and winning the American League by two games over Woodling's former team, the Indians. New York came back from a 3 games to 2 deficit to beat the Dodgers.

Woodling hit .348 with eight hits, a home run and four runs scored. In game seven, the 30-year-old Woodling led off the top of the fifth with a solo home run that tied the game at 1-1. After getting a home run from Mickey Mantle in the sixth, the Yankees went on to win 4-2 for their 15th World Series championship.

After six seasons with the Yankees, Woodling joined the Baltimore Orioles in 1955. After just 47 games with the O's, Woodling went back to Cleveland and stayed with the Indians until 1957. Woodling returned to Baltimore to play for the Orioles for three more seasons.

Woodling joined the Washington Senators in 1961. The next year, he wrapped up his career with the expansion New York Mets. Woodling batted .284 with 147 home runs and 830 RBIs in 17 seasons, and hit .318 with three homers and six RBIs in five World Series appearances. He died in 2001 at age 78 in Barberton, Ohio.

***

The World Series championship trophies continued to pile up for the Yankees in 1961 as they won their 19th Fall Classic, beating the Cincinnati Reds in five games.

But it was the first world championship for Hector Lopez, who joined the Yankees in 1959 after playing four years with the Kansas City A's. When he caught Vada Pinson's fly ball in left field in game five at Crosley Field, the 32-year-old Lopez became the first player from Panama to make the last out of the World Series.

Lopez was born on July 9, 1929 in Colon, Panama. By the time Lopez was born, Colon had over 31,000 people. Today, the sea port which is located on the Caribbean Sea coast of Panama has 204,000.

Lopez is one of several major league baseball players who were born in Colon. Among the others were Hall of Famer Rod Carew, Ben Ogilvie, Rennie Stennett and Manny Sanguillen.

Lopez began his major league career with the Kansas City A's in 1955. In each of his four full seasons in Kansas City, Lopez led American League third basemen in errors.

In May 1959, Lopez was traded to the Yankees. The next year, he was the first Panamanian-born to play in the World Series as New York faced the Pirates, but Pittsburgh won in seven thanks to a memorable walk-off home run by Bill Mazeroski. By the time Lopez joined the Yankees, he was playing in the outfield.

The Yankees won 109 games and captured the American League by eight games over Detroit in 1961. The year will be best known for Roger Maris setting the single-season home run record of 61.

Lopez played in just 93 games and hit just .222 with 54 hits in the 1961 regular season. But he shined in the World Series, hitting .333 with three hits, three runs scored and seven RBIs. He hit a two-run single in game four and homered, tripled and drove in five runs in the fifth game.

The Yankees stormed to a 6-0 lead en route to a 13-5 win over the Reds in the fifth game. With two outs in the bottom of the ninth, Lopez caught Pinson's fly ball with no runners on to give the Yankees another world championship.

Lopez also helped the Yankees win another world title in 1962, this time they beat San Francisco in a seven-game series that ended on a Willie McCovey line drive that was caught by Bobby Richardson. Lopez remained with the Yankees until 1966.

Lopez became manager of the Buffalo Bisons in 1969, becoming the first black manager in the AAA minor league level. He was manager of the Panama national team in the 2009 World Baseball Classic.

***

After the Dodgers and Giants moved to California in 1958, the Yankees became the only baseball team in New York.

That changed in 1962, when the Mets were born. The National League expanded when the Mets and the Houston Colt 45s (now the Astros) joined the league.

The Mets played at the Polo Grounds in their first two years of existence before moving to Shea Stadium in 1964. They finished with losing records in their first eight seasons, including a 40-120 mark in 1962.

But in 1969, Cleon Jones helped the Mets become a winning franchise. After catching a fly ball hit by Baltimore's Davey Johnson (who went on to manage the Mets to their second World Series title in 1986) in game five of the World Series, Jones helped the Mets win their first World Series championship and win hearts of New York City and all over the country.

The Mets came back from an eight and a half game deficit in August to capture the National League East Division title and finished their regular season with 100 wins. In 1969, Major League Baseball introduced divisional play as the National and American Leagues were split into two divisions – East and West -- and the winners of each division square off in a league championship series. The Mets advanced to the World Series against the Orioles by sweeping the Braves in three games.

Jones also turned in his best season in 1969, hitting .340 with 12 home runs and 75 RBIs and played in his first and only All-Star Game.

Long before he hit it big in New York, Jones was growing up in Mobile, Alabama. Mobile is the third-largest city in Alabama with over 194,000. When Jones was born there on August 4, 1942, Mobile's population was growing. During that time, more than 89,000 people moved to Mobile to work in the shipyards and the Brookley Army Air Field while the country was in World War II. Brookley Air Force Base was closed in 1969, the same year the Mets won the World Series.

Jones played football and baseball at Mobile County Training School, and went on to Alabama A&M University. Jones moved out of the South after signing with the Mets as an amateur free agent in 1963. For the next two years, Jones split time with the Mets and their AAA minor league team, the Buffalo Bisons.

In 1966, Jones was awarded the Mets' starting center field job. Two years later, he moved to left and his hitting blossomed, going from .205 on May 18 to finishing at .297.

In 1969, Jones batted over .300 for the first time in his major league career.

With the Mets winning it all in 1969, New York City celebrated its first baseball championship since 1962, when the Yankees beat the Giants in seven. The Miracle Mets bounced back from a first-game loss to the Orioles to win the next four games and the Series.

The Mets beat Baltimore 5-3 in the fifth game at Shea Stadium. Jones was solid at the plate in game five, getting a hit and scoring two runs. With the Orioles leading 3-0 in the sixth, Jones was struck in the foot by a Dave McNally pitch, but the umpire ruled that the ball missed Jones. After Mets manager Gil Hodges found there was a smudge of shoe polish on the ball, Jones was awarded first and later scored on a two-run homer by Series MVP Donn Clendenon. Jones also scored on a double by Ron Swoboda after leading off the eighth with a two-base hit.

With two outs in the top of the ninth and Boog Powell on first, Johnson hit a pop fly to Jones. After catching the ball on the warning track, the 27-year-old Jones dropped both of his hands and got down on one knee, then became part of a raucous celebration at Shea Stadium.

"I was saying to myself, 'Come on down, baby, come on down. It's all over,' " Jones told the Mobile (Ala.) Press-Register in 2009.

Jones helped the Mets return to the World Series in 1973, but the A's beat them in seven games. Jones stayed in New York until 1975. The next year, he wrapped up his major league career with the White Sox.

Thanks to the final out of the 1969 World Series, Jones was picked as the Mets' All-Time Left Fielder. He also was inducted into the Mets' Hall of Fame in 1991.

Jones also got some appreciation from his home state. He's a member of the Alabama Sports Hall of Fame and the Mobile Sports Hall of Fame.

***

In 1976, the Reds were unbeatable. After winning a classic 1975 World Series over the Red Sox, the Big Red Machine was looking for more in America's bicentennial year. Cincinnati got it by sweeping the Yankees in the World Series to win its second straight title.

Left fielder George Foster got the final out in game four at Yankee Stadium, catching Roy White's pop fly. With the win over the Yankees, the Reds were considered as one of the greatest teams of all time.

Like Jones, Foster also was born in Alabama. He was born on December 1, 1948 in Tuscaloosa, Alabama, home of the University of Alabama. Foster was inducted into the Alabama Sports Hall of Fame in 2002.

When he joined the Reds in 1971, Foster was playing for a team that finished fourth in the NL West with a 79-83 mark after participating in the World Series the year before.

Foster started his baseball career in 1969 with the Giants. Two years later, he made the opening day roster as the team's fourth outfielder. But shortly after the season started, Foster was sent to Cincinnati. Had he stayed in San Francisco, Foster would have played in the postseason as the Giants won the NL West championship.

But the Reds got back to their winning ways in 1972, winning 95 games, capturing the NL West title and beating the Pirates in the NLCS to advance to the World Series. Foster scored the game-winning run on a wild pitch by

Pittsburgh pitcher Bob Moose in game five of the NLCS to advance the Reds to the World Series.

With that, Foster got to play the first of his three World Series appearances. But he played in only two games.

Foster helped the Reds win it all in 1975. He hit .300 with 23 home runs and 78 RBIs.

The next year, Foster continued to blossom at the plate, hitting 29 home runs with a league-leading 121 RBIs and a .306 average. He also led NL left fielders with a .994 fielding percentage, won All-Star Game MVP honors and finished second to Morgan in the league MVP voting.

And he became a World Series champion again. Cincy clinched its fourth World Series title by beating the Yankees 7-2 in the fourth game thanks to a pair of home runs by Series MVP Johnny Bench. With no runners on and two outs in the bottom of the ninth, the 27-year-old Foster got the final out of the 1976 season by catching White's pop fly. It was Foster's final World Series game of his career.

Foster won back-to-back NL home run titles in 1977 and 1978 and earned an NL MVP award in 1977. After 10 years with the Reds, Foster joined the Mets in 1982. He split the 1986 season with the Mets and White Sox before calling it quits.

***

After winning back-to-back titles in 1975 and 1976, the Reds surpassed their intra-state rivals, the Cleveland Indians, for the most World Series championships.

The Indians have won two World Series titles, but, as of Opening Day 2014, haven't celebrated one since 1948.

That year, the Indians beat the Boston Braves in six games for their first title in 24 years.

Cleveland beat the Braves 4-3 in game six at Braves Field. Bob Kennedy recorded the final out by catching a pop fly hit by Tommy Holmes.

Photo by Baseball Digest; http://commons.wikimedia.org/wiki/File:Bob_Kennedy.png

Kennedy was born in Chicago on August 18, 1920, a day after Cleveland shortstop Ray Chapman died. Kennedy also was born on the same year the Indians won their first World Series championship.

Kennedy got to stay in his hometown to start his major league career. He joined the White Sox in September 1939 and stayed with them until 1942, when he took a three-year leave of absence from baseball to serve in the military during World War II.

Kennedy returned to the White Sox in 1946. In the 1948 midseason, Kennedy was sent to Cleveland. He hit .301 in 66 games and helped the Indians win 97 games and capture the American League crown. Cleveland beat the Red Sox in a one-game playoff to advance to the World Series against the Boston Braves.

After dropping the first game, the Indians rallied to win the World Series 4 games to 2. In the sixth game, Kennedy replaced Dale Mitchell at left with the Indians leading the Braves 4-3 with two outs in the bottom of the eighth. With no runners on and two outs in the bottom of the ninth, the 28-year-old Kennedy caught Holmes' fly ball to seal the Indians' first title in 28 years. It was Kennedy's last World Series game of his career.

Kennedy continued to play with the Indians until he was traded to the newly relocated Baltimore Orioles in 1954. He returned to the White Sox in 1955, joined the Tigers in 1956, went back to the White Sox in 1957 and finished his career with the Brooklyn Dodgers that same year. He also had managerial stints with the Cubs (1963-65) and Oakland A's (1968). Kennedy died in 2005.

***

The Dodgers played in their last season in Brooklyn in 1957 and headed west the next year. It didn't take the Dodgers long to build a championship team while they were in Los Angeles. In 1959, the Dodgers won their first title in California after beating the White Sox in six games.

Wally Moon joined the Dodgers in 1959 and was pretty valuable, earning an All-Star berth and catching the final out of the World Series at age 29.

Moon was born on April 3, 1930 in Bay, Arkansas, which is 146 miles northeast of Little Rock and has 1,800 people. He began his major league baseball career in St. Louis, which is five hours from his hometown.

Photo by Baseball Digest; http:// commons.wikimedia.org/wiki/ File:Wally_Moon_1961.png

Moon felt right at home in St. Louis in his first year in the majors in 1954, hitting .304 with 12 home runs and 76 RBIs and setting career-best marks in runs (106), hits (193), doubles (29) and stolen bases (18). The efforts earned Moon National League Rookie of the Year honors.

During Moon's five seasons in St. Louis, the Cardinals finished with just one winning season (1957). In 1959, Moon was traded to the Los Angeles Dodgers, who just completed their first season in Southern California.

Moon became a solid addition to the Dodgers, hitting .302 with 19 home runs and 74 RBIs, leading the National League in triples with 11, playing in two All-Star games (one in Pittsburgh and the other in Los Angeles) and helping the Dodgers win the National League pennant. Los Angeles came back from a seventh-place finish to win 88 games and the National League by just two games over the Milwaukee Braves, who won the league the last two years.

The Dodgers qualified for the World Series against the Chicago White Sox, who won their first American League pennant in 40 years. After getting blasted 11-0 in the first game, L.A. rallied to win the Series in six games.

The Dodgers stormed to an 8-0 lead after three and a half innings en route to a 9-3 win in the sixth game at Comiskey Park. Moon finished with six hits in the Series, including a home run in the top of the fourth in game six.

With no runners on and two outs in the bottom of the ninth, the Dodgers celebrated their second World Series title and their first in California after Moon caught Luis Aparicio's fly ball.

Moon played six more seasons with the Dodgers before retiring in 1965. He won another World Series ring as the Los Angeles beat the Twins in seven games. Moon, who now has five children and seven grandchildren, hit .289 with 142 home runs and 661 RBIs in 12-year career.

***

The Athletics got a new home in 1968.

After playing 13 seasons in Kansas City, the A's headed west to Oakland.

Things were really sunny for the A's when they moved to California. They finished with an 82-80 record in their first season in Oakland after turning in losing records in all 13 seasons at Kansas City.

When the A's won the AL West Division title in 1971, they qualified for their first postseason since 1931, when they were playing in Philadelphia.

When Joe Rudi caught Pete Rose's fly ball to left in game seven of the World Series in Cincinnati's Riverfront Stadium on October 22, 1972, the A's dynasty began.

By beating the Reds 3-2 in game seven and 4 games to 3, the A's won their first World Series title since 1930 when they were in Philly, and they won the first of their three consecutive world championships.

Besides making the final out of the World Series, Rudi turned in a solid 1972 season, leading the American League in hits with 181 and triples with nine and batting .305, four points shy of his career-best mark in 1970, and making the All-Star team.

Born on September 7, 1946 in Modesto, California, Joe Rudi began his major league career with the A's in 1967, when they were playing their final year in Kansas City. Rudi played in just 19 games.

In 1967, the A's finished last in the American League with 99 losses. Five years later, they were world champions.

Oakland picked up 93 victories and won the AL West by five games over the White Sox. The A's beat Detroit in five games in the ALCS to advance to the World Series against the Reds.

The A's took a 2 games to 0 lead after winning game two, 2-1. Rudi homered and made a famous backhanded catch of Denis Menke's smash with a runner on first.

After the Reds rallied to tie the Series at three apiece, the A's won game seven 3-2. With two outs in the bottom of the ninth, Darrel Chaney was hit by a Rollie Fingers pitch. Then, the 26-year-old Rudi caught Rose's fly ball to wrap it up.

Rudi also played on the 1973 and 1974 championship teams. He won three straight Gold Gloves from 1974-1976 and played in All-Star Games in 1974 and 1975.

Rudi stayed in Oakland until 1976. He played for the Angels from 1977-1980. He played with the Red Sox in 1981 and the A's again in 1982 before retiring with 179 home runs and 810 RBIs.

***

In 1974, Larry Herndon made his major league debut. He went on to play in the majors for 14 years, hit 107 home runs, drove in 550 runs, hit .274 and won a World Series ring.

Herndon won his World Series ring in 1984, when he helped the Tigers beat the San Diego Padres in five games for their first crown since 1968. Herndon recorded the last out of the 1984 World Series, catching a fly ball hit by future Hall of Famer Tony Gwynn.

Born in Sunflower, Mississippi, Herndon started his major league baseball career in 1974 with the Cardinals. He was drafted by the Cardinals in 1971. While playing with the Gulf Coast League Cardinals in 1971, Herndon's roommate was Randy Poffo, who went on to be known as wrestler Randy "Macho Man" Savage.

Herndon played 12 games with the Cardinals in 1974. He returned to the majors in 1976 with the Giants and played with them for six seasons. In 1982, Herndon joined the Tigers and hit a career-high 23 home runs. The next year, he hit 20 homers.

In 1984, Herndon was part of a Detroit team that roared to a 9-0 start and was 35-5 in its first 40 games. The Tigers won 104 games, which broke the franchise mark of 103 set in 1968, and captured the AL East Division title by 15 games. Detroit advanced to the World Series by sweeping Kansas City in the ALCS.

Herndon played in 125 games, hit just seven home runs after belting 43 in the last two seasons, had 43 RBIs and hit .280. He batted .333 with five hits, including a home run, in the World Series against San Diego.

In game one at San Diego, Herndon hit a two-run homer in the top of fifth to power the Tigers to a 3-2 win over the Padres. San Diego tied the Series with a game two win, but the Tigers took over from there when the Series went to Detroit. They won 5-2 in game three, 4-2 in game four and 8-4 in game five.

With two outs in the top of the ninth and San Diego catcher (and current San Francisco manager) Bruce Bochy on first, Detroit reliever Willie Hernandez got Gwynn to fly out to the 30-year-old Herndon, and Tiger fans ran onto the field as Detroit clinched its first World Series title at home since 1935.

Herndon continued to play for the Tigers until 1988 and retired after that. In 1987, he helped Detroit win the AL East Division title after hitting a solo home run over Toronto on the last day of the season. It was the only run in the 1-0 Detroit victory that clinched the Tigers the division title.

***

The Pittsburgh Pirates began the 1900s with a new manager.

Fred Clarke took over managerial duties in 1900 for Bill Watkins, who managed the Pirates for two seasons.

Clarke had a successful 16-season run as Pirates' manager, going 1,422-969 with four National League pennants and one World Series championship. He has more wins than any other manager in Pirates history (Danny Murtaugh is second with 1,115 wins). Pittsburgh finished with just two losing seasons during Clarke's tenure.

In 1909, Clarke managed the Pirates to their first of five World Series championships as Pittsburgh defeated Detroit in seven games. The Pirates have won all five of their World Series championships in seven games, their last was in 1979.

Clarke not only managed the Pirates to a world title in 1909, but he also got the final out. By catching a fly ball hit by Detroit's Tom Jones in left field in the seventh game of the Fall Classic in Detroit, Clarke became the only player-manager and the first left fielder to get the last out of the World Series.

The Pirates went through 10 managers before Clarke took over in 1900. Their history began in 1882, when they were known as the Pittsburgh Alleghenys. They changed their name to the Pirates in 1891 due to an incident that involved the Philadelphia Athletics.

Pittsburgh picked up second baseman Lou Bierbauer after Philadelphia didn't include him on its reserve list. This led to protests by the A's, and the Alleghenys' actions were claimed as "piratical." That's how the Pirates were born.

Clarke was born in Winterset, Iowa on October 3, 1872, 10 years before the Pirates were established. Winterset is a small town 37 miles southwest of Des Moines, and it's also the birthplace of actor John Wayne.

Clarke was born in a farm near Winterset. When he was two, his family moved from Iowa to Kansas as part of a covered wagon caravan before relocating to Des Moines in 1879.

When he was 20, Clarke signed his first professional contract after impressing a baseball team from Hastings, Nebraska during tryouts. He later played in the minors at Montgomery, Alabama and Savannah, Georgia before landing a job in 1894 with the Louisville Colonels, who played in the National League after playing in the American Association for several years. Clarke became player-manager for the Colonels in 1897.

After the Louisville team folded, Clarke headed to Pittsburgh in 1900. Three years later, he managed the Pirates to the first-ever World Series against the Boston Americans (now Red Sox). Boston beat Pittsburgh 5 games to 3.

In 1909, Clarke helped the Pirates turn in their best regular season in team history. Pittsburgh had 110 wins, which is a still a franchise record. Clarke turned in a strong defensive season, leading the National League left fielders in putouts (362) and fielding percentage (.987). He hit .287

with three home runs and 68 RBIs and led the league in walks with 80.

Clarke did a lot of walking in the seventh and final game against the Tigers in the 1909 World Series. Batting third in the lineup, Clarke walked a World Series record four times and scored two runs. He drew a bases-loaded walk in the top of the second.

Clarke had just four hits in the Series, two of them were home runs. He also scored seven runs, drove in seven runs and walked five times.

The Pirates cruised to an 8-0 win over the Tigers at Bennett Park, scoring two runs in the second, two in the fourth and three in the sixth. Detroit had a runner on second when Jones flied out to the 37-year-old Clarke for the last out.

Clarke continued his role as the Pirates' player-manager until 1915. He finished his career with 2,672 hits, 1,015 RBIs and a .312 batting average and 1,602 wins as manager of the Colonels and the Pirates. Clarke was inducted into the Baseball Hall of Fame in 1945. He died at Winfield, Kansas in 1960.

CHAPTER EIGHT: CENTER FIELD

In 1986, the California Angels were one strike away from going to their first World Series in franchise history.

The Angels were leading the Red Sox 5-4 with two outs and a runner on in the top of the ninth in game five in the American League Championship Series at Anaheim Stadium. The Angels were leading three games to one.

But Dave Henderson put the Angels' hopes of going to the Fall Classic on hold by hitting a two-run homer off Donnie Moore that put Boston up 6-5. The Red Sox went on to win 7-6 in 11 innings, plus the final two games to head to the World Series against the Mets.

The loss to the Red Sox devastated Angel fans for a long time.

Sixteen years later, Angel fans had reason to celebrate when center fielder Darin Erstad caught the final out in the seventh game of the Fall Classic against the Giants. The Angels, who were then known as the Anaheim Angels, won their first World Series championship with a four games to three victory over San Francisco.

"I always want to make the last out of any game because when the closer is in the game, it's always a tradition to give the ball to the closer and let him have it," Erstad said. "I thought it would be cool to be able to give (Angels reliever Troy) Percival the ball on the last game like that. Sure enough, when we were dog piling, I got to do that. Sharing it with my teammates and having that moment with Percy, that's what does it for me."

The Giants were threatening in the top of the ninth against the Angels in game seven. They were trailing 4-1 and they had runners on first and second with two outs and Kenny Lofton came to the plate, representing the tying run.

But on the first pitch, Lofton flied out to the 28-year-old Erstad to end the game and the Series.

"To be able to be the last one to touch the baseball on the last game of the season was pretty special," Erstad said. "When the ball was hit, I vividly remember my dad's voice in my head that was saying, "Use two hands." I can't say those thoughts came across my head very often, but it was in my head when the ball was in the air. It was just a cool moment. I got to share it with my dad. When it finally hits your glove, that whole experience of playing in the World Series doesn't seem real. When it hit my glove, it kind of jarred me like I just woke up. That's how mentally locked in you are for that whole thing. Once it hits your glove, I kind of like woke up and say, 'Where am I?' type of feeling. The realization of what just occurred is pretty cool."

Erstad, who is now the head baseball coach at the University of Nebraska, was a hitting machine for the Angels during the 2002 postseason, hitting .421 against the Yankees in the ALDS, .364 against Minnesota in the ALCS and .300 against the Giants.

After the game, he got a present from Percival – the game ball. It's the same ball he caught for the last out of the 2002 Series.

"Every game he saved and he saved a lot of them when we played together, he always takes the ball," Erstad said. "In that moment (after the Angels won the World Series), he said, 'You keep it.' That kind of shows you what kind of person and teammate he was. That what the kind of team we had."

The Los Angeles Angels were born in 1961 as an American League expansion team. In their first season, they played in Wrigley Field, the same ballpark that was used in the home run hitting contest TV show, *Home Run Derby*. They played their next three seasons at Dodger Stadium.

The Angels moved to Anaheim in 1965 and became the California Angels. They played in the postseason for the first time in 1979, when they played the Orioles in the ALCS after winning their first AL West championship.

The Angels won another AL West title in 1982 and came within one win away from the World Series. They lost to the Brewers in five games in the ALCS.

Four years later, the Angels won their third AL West championship, but lost to the Red Sox in the ALCS.

The Angels suffered more heartbreak in 1995, when they blew an 11-game lead in August and lost in a one-game playoff to the Mariners for the AL West championship.

Erstad joined the Angels in 1996, which was the last year the team was named the California Angels. They were known as the Anaheim Angels the next year. Erstad played 10 years with the Angels, one with the White Sox and two with the Astros before retiring in 2009. Erstad became the University of Nebraska head baseball coach in 2012.

Before starting his major league career in Southern California, Erstad was growing up in Jamestown, North Dakota. He was born there in 1974, the same year the Angels suffered their first last-place finish in franchise history.

Erstad played hockey and football and participated in track and field at Jamestown High. He played baseball for the Jamestown American Legion baseball team (Jamestown

High didn't have a baseball team). In 1992, Erstad was named the Associated Press North Dakota Athlete of the Year.

Then, Erstad became a standout for the University of Nebraska baseball team, holding the school record for career hits with 261 and earning first-team all-American honors during his three years there. The Angels selected Erstad as their No. 1 pick in the 1995 MLB Draft.

After seven years with the Angels, Erstad finally got a taste of the postseason for the first time in his career. The Angels won 99 games and finished second to Oakland in the AL West, but earned a Wild Card berth. They beat the Yankees in four games in the ALDS and the Twins in five games in the ALCS to advance to the World Series against the Giants.

By catching Lofton's fly ball in game seven of the Fall Classic, Erstad became the 10th center fielder who recorded the last out of the Fall Classic. Erstad said he's thrilled to be part of a group that included two Hall of Fame center fielders – Mickey Mantle and Joe DiMaggio.

"Every time that last out is made, I'll definitely be able to relate to those experiences and someday tell the grandkids that you did that," Erstad said. "But I'm very blessed to have an opportunity like that in my life."

Five of those center fielders made the last out in game seven of the Fall Classic, including Erstad.

****

Pepper Martin was a star in the 1931 World Series.

The Cardinals center fielder was solid at the plate in the Series against the Philadelphia Athletics, setting a World

Series record with 12 hits, including four doubles, a home run, five stolen bases and five RBIs and a .500 batting average. And he also recorded the final out of the Series, catching Max Bishop's fly ball with two outs in the top of the ninth in game seven at Sportsman's Park.

The Cardinals beat the A's 4 games to 3 to clinch their second world championship. They lost to Philadelphia in the Fall Classic the year before.

Martin played all 13 years with the Cardinals and won two World Series titles, hit .298 with 1,227 hits and 501 RBIs, won three stolen base titles and competed in four All-Star Games. He was a member of the Gashouse Gang, which is a nickname for the 1930s Cardinals teams for their aggressive play on the field.

Photo by Goudey Gum Company; http://commons. wikimedia.org/wiki/ File:PepperMartinGoudeycard.jpg

Johnny Leonard Roosevelt Martin was born on February 29, 1904 in Temple, Oklahoma. Besides Pepper, Martin has another nickname – The Wild Horse of the Osage.

Martin grew up playing baseball since he moved to Oklahoma City at age 6. At age 24, Martin began his major league career with the Cardinals. He made one appearance as a pinch runner in the 1928 World Series against the Yankees.

After playing in the minors for all of 1929 and most of 1930, Martin returned to the majors in 1931. He finished with a .300 season and helped the Cardinals pick up 101 wins and win the National League pennant by 13 games over the New York Giants.

St. Louis knocked off the Athletics 4-2 in the seventh game of the World Series. Philadelphia was threatening in the top of the ninth as it scored a pair of runs in the inning and runners on first and second with two outs.

But the A's rally – and the 1931 season – ended when Bishop flied out to the 27-year-old Martin for the last out.

Martin helped the Cardinals win another championship in 1934, when they beat the Tigers in seven games. Martin finished with 11 hits, giving him 23 in World Series play. His .418 World Series batting average is still a Series record.

Martin died on March 5, 1965 – just five days after his 61st birthday – in McAlester, Oklahoma.

***

Mickey Mantle was born 10 days after game seven of the 1931 World Series on October 20. Like Martin, Mantle grew up in Oklahoma. He ended up as one of the greatest baseball players in history, hitting 536 home runs, driving in 1,509 runs, winning three American League MVP awards and earning Triple Crown honors in 1956.

The World Series has been kind to Mantle. He holds the records for most home runs (18), RBIs (40), runs (42), walks (43) and extra-base hits (26) and total bases (123). And he recorded the final out of the World Series in 1958.

In 1957, the Yankees lost to the Milwaukee Braves in seven games. In 1958, the Yankees and Braves squared off again, this time New York won in seven games.

By Bowman Gum; http://en.wikipedia.org/wiki/File:Mickey_Mantle_1953.jpg

With the Yankees leading 6-2 and the Braves having runners on first and second with two outs in the bottom of the ninth at Milwaukee's County Stadium, Mantle caught a pop fly hit by Braves second baseman Red Schoendienst – who recorded the final out in the 1946 World Series -- in center field for the last out.

Mantle was born in Spavinaw, Oklahoma, which is a small town in the northwestern part of the state. Founded in the early 1800s, Spavinaw is 65 miles east of Tulsa, and nearby Spavinaw Lake is the main source of water for Tulsa.

When he was four, Mantle and his family moved 47 miles north to Commerce. He played baseball, football and basketball at Commerce High School.

Mantle started his major league career in 1951. By 1958, Mantle was already a star player, winning two MVP awards, going to seven All-Star Games and helping the Yankees win five World Series.

Mantle won the third of his four American League home run crowns in 1958, smacking 42 baseballs out of the park. He also helped the Yankees win 92 games and the American League by 10 games over the White Sox.

Mantle hit just .250 with six hits, two home runs, three RBIs and four runs scored in World Series. He hit both of his home runs in the second game, which was won by the Braves 13-5.

In the seventh game, the Yankees broke a 2-2 tie by scoring four runs in the top of the eighth. By getting the final out, Mantle helped New York become the first team since the Pirates in 1925 to come back from a 3 games to 1 deficit to win the World Series.

Mantle played 17 years with the Yankees until he called it quits in 1968. He was inducted to the Hall of Fame in 1974. Mantle died on August 13, 1995 in Dallas.

***

Cesar Geronimo was signed by the Yankees as a pitcher, but it didn't work out. After playing with the Astros for three seasons (1969-1971), Geronimo joined the Reds in 1972. Three years later, he was a World Champion center fielder.

Geronimo ended one of the greatest World Series of all time in 1975 by catching Carl Yastremski's fly ball in center field in game seven at Fenway Park, becoming the first player from the Dominican Republic to make the last out of the Fall Classic. The Reds beat the Red Sox in seven games for their first World Series title in 35 years.

Geronimo wasn't born the last time the Reds won it all. He was born Cesar Francisco Geronimo Zorilla on

March 11, 1948 in El Seibo, Dominican Republic. Today, Geronimo resides in Santo Domingo.

He made his major league debut with the Astros in April 1969. He played just 169 games during his three years with Houston.

But when he was traded to the Reds in 1972, Geronimo not only saw more playing time, but he became part of a winning franchise. During his nine seasons at Cincy, the Reds won two World Series titles, three National League pennants and five NL West championships. In 1975, the Reds finished with a franchise record 108 victories and won the NL West by 20 games over 1974 division champion Los Angeles.

Geronimo also demonstrated that he's a good center fielder. He won four straight Gold Glove awards from 1974 to 1977. In 1975, he led NL center fielders in putouts with 408 and double plays with five.

At the plate, Geronimo hit .257 with six home runs and 53 RBIs and a career-high 25 doubles in 1975. He hit .280 with seven hits – including a pair of home runs -- in the World Series after going hitless in 10 at-bats in the NLCS against Pittsburgh.

In game six, Geronimo hit a solo home run in the top of the sixth to give the Reds a 6-3 lead over Boston and it looked like they were going to wrap it up that night. But the Red Sox rallied with a three-run homer by Bernie Carbo in the bottom of the sixth, then got a dramatic walk-off home run by Carlton Fisk in the bottom of the 12th to win 7-6 to tie the series at three game apiece.

In the seventh game, the Reds came back from a 3-0 deficit to beat Boston 4-3. Cincinnati scored the go-ahead run in the top of the ninth on a single by Joe Morgan.

With two outs and no runners on in the bottom of the ninth, Yastremski came to the plate as one of the Red Sox's top hitters in the Series, batting .321 with a team-high nine hits. But the Red Sox veteran couldn't get the 10th hit as he flied out to the 27-year-old Geronimo for the final out.

Geronimo helped the Reds win another world championship in 1976. He helped Cincinnati return to the playoffs in 1979, but his Reds were swept by the Pirates in three games in the NLCS. Geronimo was the last out of the series after Pittsburgh pitcher Bert Byleven got him on a called third strike.

After playing the 1980 season with the Reds, Geronimo played three seasons with the Royals before retiring. He was inducted into the Reds' Hall of Fame in 2008.

***

The Baltimore Orioles began the 1970s with a World Series championship over Cincinnati in 1970.

In 1979, the Orioles had their sights set on ending the 1970s with a championship. But Pittsburgh center fielder Omar Moreno had other ideas.

After catching Pat Kelly's fly ball with no runners on for the final out in the seventh game of the 1979 World Series at Memorial Stadium, Moreno helped the Pirates win their fifth world championship. Pittsburgh won 4-1 to win the Series 4 games to 3 after being down 3 games to 1.

The 1979 World Series championship was an early birthday present for Moreno. Pittsburgh won game seven just a week before Moreno's 27th birthday.

Omar Renan Moreno Quintero was born on Oct. 24, 1952 in Puerto Armuelles, Panama. Founded in 1928,

Puerto Armuelles is a city on Panama's Pacific Coast with a population of 24,900. Puerto Armuelles was named in honor of one of the heroes of the Coto War, Tomas Armuelles, who was a member of the Panamanian Defensive Forces who died in an accident in 1921 during the war between Panama and Costa Rica.

Moreno is the most famous citizen in Puerto Armuelles. Today, he lives in Panama, as he and his wife have run the Omar Moreno Foundation, a youth baseball charity for underprivileged kids in Panama.

By catching Pat Kelly's pop fly in the 1979 World Series, Moreno became the first Panamanian player since Hector Lopez in 1961 to make the final out of the World Series.

Inspired by Sister Sledge's disco tune, "We Are Family," the Pirates won 98 games, edged Montreal by two games to win the NL East and advanced to the World Series by sweeping Cincinnati in the NLCS.

Moreno was a stolen base king in 1979. By stealing 77 bases, Moreno led the National League in thefts for the second year in a row. He also hit .282 with eight home runs, 69 RBIs and a career-high 110 runs scored, and was first in the National League in at-bats with 695.

Moreno didn't steal any bases in the Fall Classic against the Orioles, but turned in a solid offensive showing, hitting .333 with 11 hits, three RBIs and four runs scored.

With the Pirates leading 2-1 in the top of the ninth in the seventh game, Moreno added two insurance runs for the Pirates by smacking an RBI single and scoring a run after Bill Robinson was hit by a pitch. Pittsburgh took the 2-1 lead on a two-run shot by Series MVP Willie Stargell in the sixth.

Pittsburgh reliever Kent Tekulve retired the side in the bottom of the ninth. On the first pitch from Tekulve, Kelly popped up to Moreno for the final out.

Moreno played in his first and only World Series in 1979. He joined the Pirates in September 1975, and stayed with the team until 1982.

Moreno joined the Astros in 1983, but was traded to the Yankees later that year. After being released by the Yankees in August 1985, Moreno joined the Royals for the final month of the season. Moreno wasn't on the Royals postseason roster in 1985, the year Kansas City won its first World Series title.

After playing with the Braves in 1986, Moreno retired with 1,257 hits and 486 stolen bases.

***

In 1979, the Orioles made their fifth World Series appearance since moving from St. Louis in 1954. They were first known as the St. Louis Browns. Before they were the St. Louis Browns, they were the Milwaukee Brewers.

The Brewers were established in 1891, but 12 years later, they moved to St. Louis and changed their name to the St. Louis Browns, which was in reference to the original name of the 1880s club that by 1900 was known as the Cardinals.

The Browns made their first and only World Series appearance in 1944, but lost to their city rivals, the Cardinals in six games. It was during a time when most major league players joined or got drafted by the military due to World War II.

Bill Veeck bought the Browns in 1951. Two years later, he attempted to move the Browns in Baltimore. In 1954, the

Browns headed east to Maryland and became the Baltimore Orioles, making St. Louis a one-baseball team town. That year, Paul Blair was a 10-year-old from Oklahoma trying to accomplish his dream of becoming a professional baseball player.

The Orioles lost 100 games in their first season in Baltimore. They didn't get their first winning season until 1960. In 1964, Hank Bauer took over managing duties in Baltimore, and Blair joined the team in September of that season.

Blair, who was drafted by the Orioles in the 1962 first-year draft, won a starting job in center field in 1965. The next year, he helped Baltimore win its first American League pennant since moving to Maryland in 1954.

The Orioles won 97 games, which tied their mark from 1964. After back-to-back third-place finishes in the American League the last two years, the Orioles came out on top in 1966, sweeping 1965 World Champion Los Angeles in four games.

The Orioles won the fourth game 1-0 at Memorial Stadium on a home run by Series MVP Frank Robinson in the bottom of the fourth.

The 22-year-old Blair came in the top of the eighth to play center field. He robbed Jim Lefebvre a home run that would have tied the game.

One inning later, the Dodgers were threatening with runners on first and second and two outs. But Blair – an eight-time Gold Glove winner -- caught Lou Johnson's fly ball to end the Dodgers' rally, the game and the Series.

The day before in game three, Blair hit a solo home run off Claude Osteen, his only hit in the World Series.

Blair won three more World Series rings. He helped the O's win it again in 1970. Then, he went to the Yankees in 1977 and helped them win back-to-back titles in 1977 and 1978. Blair also played in the World Series in 1969 and 1971, but his Orioles lost both years. After retiring in 1980 with the Yanks, Blair finished with 134 home runs, 620 RBIs and a .250 batting average.

***

After losing the World Series in 1974, 1977 and 1978, the Dodgers were back on top in 1981, beating the Yankees in six games. Los Angeles won the sixth game 9-2 at Yankee Stadium, and Ken Landreaux got the final out of the Series by catching a fly ball hit by Yankee first baseman Bob Watson.

Landreaux was born in Los Angeles on Dec. 22, 1954 in Los Angeles, four years before the Brooklyn Dodgers moved west. Today, he's teaching young children how to play baseball at the Urban Youth Academy in nearby Compton.

Landreaux was drafted by the Houston Astros in the eighth round after graduating from high school in nearby Compton in the early 1970s, but decided to play college baseball at Arizona State and helped the Sun Devils reach the College World Series in 1975 and 1976.

Landreaux returned to California after being selected by the Angels in the 1976 amateur draft. He played a combined 116 games in two seasons in Anaheim in 1977 and 1978 before being traded to the Twins in 1979.

Landreaux's offense blossomed in Minnesota, setting career marks in home runs (15), RBIs (83) and batting average (.305) in 1979 and setting a team record 31-game hitting streak in 1980.

Landreaux's stay with the Twins was short-lived. He went back to Los Angeles in 1981, when he was traded to the Dodgers. He stayed with the Dodgers until 1987, when he retired.

But Landreaux's first season with the Dodgers was interrupted with the two-month strike that started on June 12 and ended on August 9. Owners and players couldn't agree on the direction of free agent compensation, forcing baseball to go on strike.

After the strike ended in August, a total of 713 games were cancelled, equating to 38 percent of Major League Baseball's schedule. With that, the owners decided to split the 1981 schedule, with the first-place teams in each half in each division play each other in a best-of-five division series. The four winners advance to the best of five League Championship Series.

The Dodgers finished second overall in the National League West with a 63-47 record, but won the first half with a 36-21 mark, so they had already clinched a berth for the playoffs. They played the Astros, who won the second half, in a best of five NL West Division series. The Dodgers won that playoff 3 games to 2 to advance to the NLCS against the Expos, who beat the 1980 world champion Phillies in the NL East Division series.

The Dodgers beat the Expos in five games to advance to the World Series against the Yankees. Rick Monday hit a dramatic solo home run in the top of the ninth to give the Dodgers a 2-1 win in game five.

The Dodgers came back from a 2 games to none deficit to beat the Yankees in the World Series. With Willie Randolph on second and Reggie Jackson on first, Los Angeles reliever got Bob Watson to fly out to the 26-year-old Landreaux on a 1-0 pitch.

Landreaux struggled offensively in 1981, hitting .251 in the regular season and getting a combined six hits in the three series against the Astros, Expos and Yankees. But he shined on defense as he didn't make any errors in center field.

Landreaux never played in another World Series. He helped the Dodgers win NL West titles in 1983 and 1985, but the team lost to the Phillies and Cardinals, respectively.

***

Major League Baseball went through another major work stoppage in 1994, but this time the strike wiped out the postseason and the World Series, marking the first time since 1904 that the Fall Classic wasn't played.

The 1994 strike began on August 12. During the negotiation of a new collective bargaining agreement, the players refused to agree on a salary cap that was proposed by the owners, setting up the eighth work stoppage in Major League Baseball history.

The strike put a big dent into the Montreal Expos' best season in team history. They had the best record in baseball at 74-40 and were six games ahead of the Braves in the National League East. The last time Montreal was in the postseason was in 1981, when Major League Baseball had a long strike.

Marquis Grissom was one of the Montreal players in the 1994 season. The Atlanta native joined the Expos in August 1989 after being selected by the team in the third round of the MLB draft the year before. As the Expos' leadoff hitter and center fielder, Grissom became valuable, leading the National League in stolen bases twice, played in the All-Star Game twice and won four straight Gold Gloves. He also recorded the final out in Dennis Martinez's perfect game against the Dodgers in 1991.

In 1994, Grissom was hitting .288 with 11 home runs and 45 RBIs and was leading the National League in plate appearances with 521 before the strike. After the strike, Grissom headed south to Atlanta.

Because of financial reasons, the Expos were forced to trade many of their stars, including Grissom. He was traded the Braves in exchange for three players. The trade gave Grissom an opportunity to play in his hometown and play for a team that has been a baseball powerhouse.

The Braves played in back-to-back World Series in 1991 and 1992, but lost both of them to Minnesota and Toronto, respectively. They also won three consecutive National League East division titles from 1991 to 1993 and were on top of the division again in 1995.

The Braves moved to Atlanta in 1966, a year before Grissom was born. They won the National League West division crown in 1969 and placed first in the division again in 1982. Thanks to their televised games on Superstation WTBS, the Braves were getting national exposure and were known as America's Team.

Before they started their successful run in 1991, the Braves had their share of futility, finishing with seven consecutive losing seasons. They finished last in the National League West in 1990, but came out on top in 1991.

In 1995, the Braves came out on top in the World Series, beating the Cleveland Indians four games to two. Thanks to a solo home run by David Justice, Atlanta beat Cleveland 1-0 in the sixth game at Atlanta-Fulton County Stadium. The Braves became the first team to win the World Series in three different cities.

Atlanta had another reason to celebrate as Grissom made the final out in front of his hometown fans. The center fielder caught a fly ball hit by Carlos Baerga and celebrated his first World Series championship after all the disappointment he went through the previous year.

Grissom hit .258 with 12 home runs and 42 RBIs in his first season with the Braves in 1995. He became the first center fielder to record the final out of the World Series since Landreaux in 1981.

Grissom didn't get another World Series ring. He played in the World Series in 1996 and 1997, but his teams fell short. The Braves lost to the Yankees in six games in 1996. In 1997, Grissom was sent to the Indians, but his new team lost to the Marlins in seven games.

Grissom played for the Brewers, Dodgers and Giants before retiring in March 2006. Today, he resides in College Park, Georgia, an Atlanta suburb.

***

By winning their first World Series title in 1995, the Braves were a step away from claiming themselves as the team of the 1990s.

Then, the Yankees took over.

The Bronx Bombers won World Series titles in the next four seasons – including two over Atlanta -- to claim themselves as the best team of the 1990s. They also won it all in 2000 after beating the Mets in five games in the Subway Series.

During his 15 years with the Yankees, center fielder Bernie Williams played on four world championship teams, including the one in 2000.

The 32-year-old Williams recorded the final out in the 2000 World Series, catching a pop fly hit by Mets catcher Mike Piazza with a runner on third in the fifth game. The Yankees beat the Mets 4-2 on a two-run single by Luis Sojo in the top of the ninth.

Williams is one of 10 players from outside the United States who made the last out of the World Series. The others are Bert Campaneris (Cuba), Robinson Cano (Dominican Republic),

Photo by Daniel Hartwig; http://en.wikipedia.org/wiki/ File:Bernie_Williams_2004.jpg

Geronimo (Dominican Republic), Jackie Hernandez (Cuba), Hector Lopez (Panama), Dolf Luque (Cuba), Moreno (Panama), Juan Uribe (Dominican Republic) and Koji Uehara (Japan).

Bernabe Williams Figueroa was born on September 13, 1968 in San Juan, Puerto Rico. The Williams family lived in the Bronx until Bernie was 1 year old, when they moved to Puerto Rico.

Before beginning his major league career in 1991, Williams was a standout in track and field, winning gold medals in four events in the Central American and Caribbean Junior Championships in 1984, at age 16.

Williams joined the Yankees in 1991. He played in 85 ganes and batted .238 with three home runs and 34 RBIs. Williams finished in double digits in home runs for 14 straight years (1993-2006) and won a batting title in 1998, hitting .339.

In 2000, Williams set career marks in home run s (30) and RBIs (121) and won his fourth and final Gold Glove award. As for the Yankees, they won 87 games, edged Boston by 2.5 games to win the American League East Division and knocked off the A's in the ALDS and the Mariners in the ALCS to advance to their third straight World Series.

Williams had just two hits in the World Series against the Mets. He still turned in a solid career in postseason play, ranking first in RBIs (80) and second in home runs (22), doubles (29), total hits (128), total bases (223 and runs scored (83).

Williams retired in 2006 with a .297 batting average, 287 home runs, 1,257 RBIs, 1,366 runs scored and 449 doubles. He also was a five-time All-Star and won four Gold Glove awards.

***

The 2000 World Series between the Yankees and Mets marked the first postseason Subway Series since 1956. DiMaggio knows a lot about playing in the Subway Series – he played in six of them.

One of them came in 1941, when the Yankees played the Brooklyn Dodgers in the Fall Classic. On the same year he set a major-league record 56-game hitting streak, DiMaggio helped the Bronx Bombers beat the Dodgers in five games.

It was also fitting that DiMaggio recorded the final out of the Series. He caught a pop fly hit by Jimmy Wasdell -- who was pinch hitting for Pee Wee Reese -- with no one on base in the bottom of the ninth for the last out of the 1941 season.

The Yankees beat the Dodgers 3-1 in the fifth game at Ebbets Field. It was the first time the two teams met in the World Series.

DiMaggio was 36 years old when the Yankees won it all in 1941. When he retired 10 years later, DiMaggio won a total of nine world championships.

DiMaggio's baseball life began in the San Francisco Bay Area. He was born in Martinez, California, which is north of Oakland, and moved to San Francisco when he was 1 year old. DiMaggio started playing pro ball in 1932, when he played for the San Francisco Seals of the Pacific Coast League. A year later, he had a PCL-record 61-game hitting streak.

DiMaggio started his major league career in 1936 with the Yankees. He helped the Bronx Bombers win four straight World Series from 1936-1939.

DiMaggio helped the Yankees return to the World Series in 1941 after a 1-year absence. He hit .357 with 30 home runs and an American League leading 125 RBIs, won American League MVP honors and led the Yankees to a 101-win season. DiMaggio's 56-game hitting streak began on May 15 against the White Sox and ended on July 17 against the Indians.

DiMaggio hit .263 with five hits in the 1941 World Series. In 10 Fall Classic appearances, DiMaggio hit .271 with eight home runs and 30 RBIs. He ended his career on top in 1951 as the Yankees beat the New York Giants in the World Series.

DiMaggio finished with 361 home runs, 1,537 RBIs, 2,214 hits and a .325 batting average and three American League MVP awards. He was inducted to the Baseball Hall of Fame in 1955. DiMaggio died on March 8, 1999 at age 84 in Hollywood, Florida.

CHAPTER NINE: RIGHT FIELD

After winning seven American League West Division titles, two league pennants and participating in five of the last 10 ALCS, the Kansas City Royals finally captured their first World Series title on October 27, 1985.

It was also a night to remember for right fielder Darryl Motley.

First, Motley belted a two-run homer off St. Louis pitcher John Tudor in the bottom of the second in game seven of the I-70 Fall Classic between the Royals and Cardinals at Royals Stadium. Then in the top of the ninth, he did something no right fielder had done in 34 years – get the final out of the World Series.

Motley caught a high pop fly hit by Andy Van Slyke with no runners on to give the Royals their first championship since joining the majors in 1969.

The Royals were one of four expansion teams in 1969. The Montreal Expos, the San Diego Padres and the Seattle Pilots (now Milwaukee Brewers) were the others. Major League Baseball returned to Kansas City after a one-year hiatus.

After the 1967 season, the Kansas City Athletics moved to Oakland after 13 seasons. So there was no baseball in K.C. in 1968.

The A's moved to Kansas City in 1955 after playing in Philadelphia for 53 years. Charlie Finley bought the club in 1960, the same year Motley was born.

Motley was born on January 21, 1960 in Muskogee, Oklahoma. When Motley was 11 months old, Finley bought the A's. The A's weren't successful during their stay in Kansas City as they finished with a losing record in all 13 seasons.

Finley moved the A's to Oakland, where they immediately became a powerhouse, winning three World Series titles, three American League championships and five AL West crowns in their first eight seasons.

The Royals lost 190 games in their first two seasons. Then, they became a powerhouse, winning three consecutive AL West Division titles from 1976-78 and capturing their first American League pennant in 1980.

In the strike-shortened 1981 season, Motley joined the Royals. Three years later, Motley turned in a solid offensive season, setting career-best marks in RBIs (70), doubles (24), hits (148) and batting average (.284). He also helped the Royals win the AL West, but they were swept by the eventual World Champion Tigers in three games in the ALCS.

The next year, Motley hit a career-high 17 home runs, but his averaged slipped to .222. Still, he played a key role in helping the Royals win another AL West championship. Kansas City won 91 games to edge the California Angels by one game in the division standings.

Then, the Royals came back from a 3 games to 1 deficit to beat Toronto in the ALCS, setting up an all-Show Me State World Series against the Cardinals which will be best known for the blown call by first base umpire Don Denkinger in the bottom of the ninth of game six that helped the Royals win 2-1 to set up a seventh game.

The seventh game was scoreless when Motley came up to the plate in the bottom of the second. On a 3-2 pitch,

Motley hit a foul ball into the left field seats. When he found out it was foul, Motley slammed his bat and cracked it. A bat boy gave the 25-year-old Motley a new bat, and Motley followed with the two-run shot to give Kansas City a 2-0 lead it would relinquish. The Royals went on to win 11-0.

Motley hit .364 with four hits in the Fall Classic. By making the final out in game seven, Motley helped Series MVP Bret Saberhagen record a five-hit shutout over St. Louis.

The Royals haven't returned to the postseason since winning the 1985 World Series. As of Opening Day 2014, at 29 years, the Royals have the longest current postseason drought than any other team.

As for Motley, he split the 1986 season with the Royals and Braves. He played just six games with Atlanta in 1987 before his major league career ended.

Motley is one of six right fielders who recorded the final out of the World Series. The last one to do that was Hank Bauer.

***

Bauer played baseball in Kansas City. He played his final two seasons with the Kansas City Athletics in 1960 and 1961. He also was the team's manager from 1961-1962.

Before heading to K.C., Bauer played 10 years with the Yankees. He helped the Yankees win seven world titles, including in 1951, when he got the final out in game six of the Fall Classic against the New York Giants at Yankee Stadium.

With two outs in the top of the ninth and the Yankees leading 4-3, the Giants had the tying run on second base. Sal Yvars, who came in to pinch hit for Hank Thompson, lined out to Bauer for the final out. The Yankees won the Series four games to two.

Bauer was born in East St. Louis, Illinois – right across the Mississippi from St. Louis -- on July 31, 1922. Bauer is among a list of numerous famous athletes who were born in East St. Louis that includes Jackie Joyner-Kersee, Bryan Cox, Cuonzo Martin and

By Bowman Gum; http:// commons.wikimedia.org/wiki/ File:Hank_Bauer_1953.jpg

Jimmy Connors. He played baseball and basketball at East St. Louis Central Catholic High.

Before beginning his major league career in 1948, Bauer earned two Bronze Stars and two Purple Hearts for fighting for his country while serving in the Marine Corps.

After playing just 19 games in his first year in the majors, Bauer's playing time increased, and so did his productivity at the plate. He finished in double digits in home runs for 10 straight seasons. After he retired as a player in 1961, Bauer hit .277 with 164 home runs and 703 RBIs.

In 1951, Bauer and the Yankees won 98 games and the American League pennant by five games over Cleveland to advance to the World Series against the Giants, who won the National League pennant on a dramatic home run by Bobby Thomson in a one-game playoff against the Brooklyn Dodgers at the Polo Grounds.

In game six, the 29-year-old Bauer not only made the final out, but he came up big at the plate, smacking bases-loaded triple in the bottom of the sixth that broke a 1-1 tie. It was one of just three hits for Bauer in the Fall Classic.

Bauer stayed with the Yankees until 1959. Then, he was traded to Kansas City for Roger Maris, who set the single-season home run record in 1961.

In addition to the Kansas City A's, Bauer also managed the Orioles for four years – which included a World Series championship in 1966 – and the Oakland A's for one year. Bauer died on February 9, 2007 at age 84 in Lenexa, Kansas.

***

Ben Chapman was another Yankee right fielder who caught the final out of the World Series. In 1932 against the Cubs, Chapman caught a fly ball hit by Riggs Stephenson in game four to help the Yankees complete the four-game sweep.

It was Chapman's only World Series championship of his 16-year baseball career. He played for seven different teams and played in only one World Series, which was in 1932.

In game four of the Fall Classic against the Cubs at Wrigley Field, the Yankees came back from a 4-1 first-inning deficit to win 13-6 and their fourth world championship.

With no runners on base, the Yankees' Herb Pennock got Stephenson to fly out to the 23-year-old Chapman for the final out.

Chapman batted .294 with five hits and six RBIs in the Series. In the fourth game, he drove in the Yankees' 13th run with a double that scored Bill Dickey.

Chapman stole 38 bases in 1932 to lead the American League in thefts for the second straight year. He had 287 stolen bases in his career.

Chapman batted over .300 in his first five seasons with the Yankees. The only exception came in 1932, when he hit .299.

Chapman was born on Christmas Day 1908 in Nashville, Tennessee. He started his major league baseball career in 1930 with the Yankees. After playing in the infield – and leading the American League in errors with 24 -- in his first season, Chapman moved to the outfield in 1931.

In 1932, Chapman helped the Yankees win 107 games and the American League pennant by 13 games over the Philadelphia A's, who won the league championship the last three years. Chapman was part of a Yankee team that included Babe Ruth, Lou Gehrig, Bill Dickey and Lefty Gomez.

Chapman stayed with the Yankees until 1936. That same year, he went to the Washington Senators. He also played with the Red Sox (1937-38), Indians (1939-40), the Senators again (1941), White Sox (1941), Dodgers (1944-1945) and Phillies (1945-46). He played in the All-Star Game for four straight years (1933-36).

Chapman became player-manager for the Phillies in 1945 and stayed as manager until 1948. While at Philadelphia, Chapman was best known for his attempts to intimidate

Jackie Robinson, who became the first African-American to play in the major leagues in 1947. During a series between the Dodgers and Phillies, Chapman instructed his pitchers to bean Robinson instead of walking him whenever they had a 3-0 count on him. The plans backfired.

Chapman died on July 7, 1993 at age 84 in Hoover, Alabama.

***

After a 16-year drought, the Philadelphia A's were back on top, winning back-to-back World Series titles in 1929 and 1930.

They can thank Bing Miller for that.

In 1929, the six-foot-tall, 185-pound right fielder delivered a two-out, walk-off double in the bottom of the ninth in Game 5 that gave the A's a 3-2 win and clinched them their fourth World Series title.

In 1930, Miller became the second right fielder to record the last out of the World Series after he caught a fly ball hit by the Cardinals' Jimmie Wilson in the sixth game at Philadelphia. The A's beat St. Louis 7-1 to win 4 games to 2 and their fifth World Series title.

Edmund John Miller was born on August 30, 1894 in Vinton, Iowa, which is outside Cedar Rapids. He started his major league career in 1921 with the Washington Senators, but was traded to Philadelphia the next year.

Miller played with the St. Louis Browns in 1926 and 1927 before returning to the A's in 1928 and helped them get back on the championship track.

In 1930, Miller hit .303 and drove in a career-high 100 runs to help the A's win their second straight American League pennant. Philadelphia won 102 games.

In the sixth game of the World Series against the Cardinals at Shibe Park in Philly, the A's stormed to a 7-0 lead after six innings. St. Louis scored a run in the top of the ninth and runners on first and second with two outs when Wilson flied out to the 36-year-old Miller to the final out.

Miller had just three hits in the Series, including two in the sixth game. He hit .368 in the 1929 Series.

Miller helped the A's win another American League pennant in 1931, but they lost to the Cardinals in seven. Then, Philadelphia hit another drought and would not make the postseason again until 1971, when the A's were playing in Oakland.

As for Miller, he continued to play for the Philadelphia A's until 1934. He played for the Red Sox in 1935 and 1936 before retiring with 116 home runs, 992 RBIs and a .311 batting average.

Miller died on May 7, 1966 at age 71 in Philadelphia from complications of injuries from a car accident while driving home from a Phillies game.

***

In 1913, Philadelphia A's right fielder Eddie Murphy – not the famous actor-comedian -- recorded the last out of the World Series against the Giants. Murphy, who was nicknamed "Honest Eddie," caught a fly ball hit by Larry Doyle with no runners on base in the bottom of the ninth in the fifth game to clinch Philadelphia's third world title in four seasons. Murphy also had two hits and scored a run in the fifth game, which was won by the A's 3-1.

Just like the actor-comedian Eddie Murphy, the baseball player Eddie Murphy was born in New York State. He was born John Edward Murphy on October 2, 1891 in Hancock, a town in Delaware County that is located 154 miles north of New York City.

After playing minor league ball with the Baltimore Orioles, Murphy was traded to the A's in 1912. He hit .317 in 33 games and earned him a regular spot in right field for Philadelphia the next year.

In 1913, Murphy hit .295 with a career-best 105 runs scored. He also helped the A's win their third American League pennant in four years. The A's won 96 games to advance to the World Series against the Giants.

Philadelphia won the Series four games to one. In game five at Polo Grounds on Oct. 11, 1913, just nine days after Murphy's 22nd birthday, the A's scored a run in the first and two in the third. Besides being the first right fielder to record the final out of the World Series, Murphy finished with five hits and two runs scored in the five games against the Giants.

Murphy stayed with the A's until 1915, when he went to the White Sox. In 1919, he went back to the World Series as the White Sox won the American League pennant, but lost to the Reds. Eight Chicago players were banned for throwing the Series, but Murphy wasn't one of them, earning him the nickname, "Honest Eddie."

Murphy stayed with the White Sox until 1921. He played one more season in 1926 with the Pirates before retiring with 680 hits, 111 stolen bases and a .287 batting average.

Murphy died on Feb. 21, 1969 at age 77 in Dunmore, Pennsylvania. During that time, Eddie Murphy – the actor/comedian – was living in foster care while growing up in Brooklyn. He said in interviews that staying in foster care helped him developed his sense of humor, which made him become the famous entertainer he is today.

***

The National Baseball Hall of Fame began in 1936 with five inductees, Ty Cobb, Babe Ruth, Honus Wagner, Christy Mathewson and Walter Johnson.

Twenty more players were inducted when the Hall of Fame Museum was built in 1939. As of Opening Day 2014, a total of 300 players have been inducted to Cooperstown. Out of those 300 individuals, 21 of them made the last out of the World Series.

New York Giants right fielder Ross Youngs was one of them. In the fifth game between the Giants and Yankees, the 25-year-old Youngs caught Aaron Ward's fly ball in the fifth game to help the Giants win their second straight World Series championship. The Giants beat the Yankees 5-3 to win the Series four games to none and a tie.

Youngs played 10 seasons (1917-1926) in the majors, all of them were with the Giants. He was a terrific hitter, finishing with nine .300 seasons, including eight in a row.

Youngs' career was cut short in 1926, when he was diagnosed with a kidney disease called Bright's disease. Other famous people such as Hall of Fame baseball player Ty Cobb and poet Emily Dickenson also had the disease.

Youngs died on October 22, 1927 at age 30 in San Antonio, Texas. He finished his baseball career with a .322 batting average, 812 runs scored, 592 RBIs and 153 stolen bases and two World Series championships during his career. The strong numbers impressed the Hall of Fame Veteran's Committee, and Youngs was inducted to Cooperstown in 1972.

Besides Youngs, Bob Gibson, Rollie Fingers, Bruce Sutter, Sandy Koufax, Mickey Mantle, Eddie Mathews, Pee Wee Reese, Red Schoendienst, Joe DiMaggio, Lou Gehrig, Babe Ruth, Frank Baker, Joe Sewell, Joe Gordon, Leo Durocher, Brooks Robinson, Joe Tinker, Eddie Collins, George "High Pockets" Kelly and Cal Ripken, Jr. are the other Hall of Fame players who made the last out of the World Series.

Royce Middlebrook Youngs was born on April 10, 1897 in Shiner, Texas, which is known as the "Cleanest Little City in Texas." Youngs and his family later moved 92 miles west to San Antonio.

Youngs began his major league career in 1917 with the Giants. He earned a full-time job as the team's right fielder the next year.

Youngs turned in a solid regular season in 1922, hitting .331 with seven home runs and 86 RBIs and leading National League right fielders in assists with 28.

Youngs also was solid at the plate in the 1922 Fall Classic, hitting .375 with six hits, two runs scored and two RBIs. He scored both of his runs in the fifth game.

By the making the final out in the fifth game, Youngs helped the Giants become the first National League team since the Cubs in 1907-08 to win back-to-back World Series titles. New York advanced to the World Series by winning 93 games and the National League championship by seven games over Cincinnati, becoming the first team to win 10 National League crowns.

CHAPTER TEN: THE OTHER SIDE

On November 15, 2012, Miguel Cabrera added another honor to his outstanding baseball career. He was named the American League Most Valuable Player, making it the second year in a row a Detroit Tiger won the biggest honor in baseball.

Cabrera earned MVP honors after hitting .330 with 44 home runs and 139 runs batted in and helped the Tigers reach the World Series.

Even though Cabrera was thrilled to win a big award, he was still upset that he made the final out of the 2012 World Series.

"It's very sad, what we're feeling right now," Cabrera told the USA Today after game four of the World Series. "I feel embarrassed. I struck out. I made the last out in the World Series."

Still, the final out would not erase Cabrera's outstanding career. Cabrera played in seven all-star games, won two batting titles, two RBI championships, two home run crowns and two MVP awards (He won another MVP award in 2013). He has over 1,900 hits with over 300 home runs and is hitting over .300 for his career, so he has Hall of Fame potential.

If Cabrera goes to Cooperstown, he'll join 12 Hall of Famers who made the final out of the World Series. He'll join a list that includes Babe Ruth, Carl Yastremski, Honus Wagner, Goose Goslin, Luis Aparicio, Frankie Frisch, Earl

Averill, Pee Wee Reese, Red Schoendienst, Jackie Robinson, Willie McCovey and Tony Gwynn.

Tony Gwynn was the last Hall of Famer to make the final out of the World Series. Gwynn was in his third season in a San Diego Padre uniform when he flied out to Detroit left fielder Larry Herndon in the fifth game of the 1984 World Series at Tiger Stadium. That year, Gwynn won the batting title with a .351 batting average, played in his first All-Star game at San Francisco and helped the Padres win their first National League championship.

Gwynn was inducted to the Hall of Fame in 2007 after turning in a solid 20-year career that included eight batting championships and 15 trips to the All-Star Game. He did return to the World Series in 1998, but the Padres were swept by the Yankees, so Gwynn didn't receive any World Series rings during his career.

Yastremski flied out to Cincinnati center fielder Cesar Geronimo for the final out in game seven of the 1975 World Series. Fourteen years later, the Boston Red Sox outfielder was inducted to Cooperstown after hitting .285 with 452 home runs and 3,419 hits in his 22 years at Beantown. He won a Triple Crown and American League MVP award in 1967 and played in 18 All-Star games, including a 1970 contest where he won MVP honors. Yastremski also never won a World Series title.

Willie McCovey could have won a World Series championship had his line drive was about a few feet higher than New York second baseman Bobby Richardson's glove in game seven of the 1962 World Series. But when McCovey's drive was caught by Richardson, the Giants lost to the Yankees in seven games, and that as close as McCovey would get to a World Series title.

That year, McCovey played in his fourth major league season. He ended up playing 21 seasons, most of them were in San Francisco (McCovey also had stints in San Diego and Oakland). After retiring in 1980, McCovey finished with 2,211 hits, 521 home runs and 1,555 RBIs, six All-Star game appearances, a Rookie of the Year award in 1959 and a National League MVP award in 1969. All of those accomplishments helped McCovey earn a trip to Cooperstown in 1986.

The same year McCovey won Rookie of the Year honors, Luis Aparicio made the final out of the 1959 World Series against the Dodgers by flying out to Los Angeles left fielder Wally Moon.

The Chicago White Sox shortstop went on to turn in a solid 17-year career, hitting .262 with 2,677 hits and 791 runs batted in, making 13 trips to the All-Star game and earning nine Gold Gloves. He also won a Rookie of the Year award in 1956, the same year Robinson retired from baseball.

Robinson's career ended on a down note in the 1956 World Series, when Yankee pitcher Johnny Kucks struck out the famous Brooklyn Dodgers second baseman for the final out in game seven. After the season, Robinson was traded to the New York Giants, but the trade never happened.

Robinson became the first African-American to play in the major leagues in 1947. After nine years, Robinson won a Rookie of the Year, an MVP award and a batting title and earned six trips to the All-Star game. He was inducted to the Baseball Hall of Fame in 1962.

Another Hall of Fame second baseman, Schoendienst, played on two World Series championship teams in 1946 with the Cardinals and in 1957 with the Milwaukee Braves.

He recorded the final out of the 1946 World Series. But in 1958, Schoendienst came up short of his third World Series ring as he made the final out of the World Series against the Yankees by flying out to Mickey Mantle in center field. Schoendienst was inducted to the Hall in 1989.

Pee Wee Reese helped the Brooklyn Dodgers their first World Series title in 1955. Before 1955, Reese had played in five World Series, but he couldn't get the big one. In 1952, he made the final out of the Fall Classic against the Yankees by flying out to Yankee left fielder Gene Woodling in the seventh game. Reese was voted by the Veterans' Committee to earn a trip to the Hall of Fame in 1984.

Another Hall of Fame Veterans' Committee selection, Earl Averill, played in his first and only World Series in 1940 while he was a member of the Detroit Tigers. But Averill's only World Series trip ended on a disappointing note – he made the final out.

In the seventh game against the Reds, Averill grounded out to second to end Detroit's hopes of winning its second World Series title. Averill went 0-for-3 in pinch-hit attempts, including the one in game seven.

Averill retired the next year. A center fielder, Averill also played with the Indians and Boston Braves, hit .318 with 238 home runs and 1,164 RBIs and went to the All-Star Game six times. He was inducted into the Hall of Fame in 1975, just eight years before he died. Averill once said, "Had I been elected after my death, I had made arrangements that my name never be placed in the Hall of Fame."

After winning two World Series championships as a member of the New York Giants, Frankie Frisch was setting his sights on winning his first title with the Cardinals in 1928. But those hopes were diminished when he flied out to Babe Ruth in foul territory near left field in game four of the Fall Classic against the Yankees.

Frisch went to win not one, but two championships in St. Louis in 1931 and 1934, when the Cardinals beat the Philadelphia A's and the Tigers, respectively.

Frisch played in the All-Star Game three times, earned National League MVP honors in 1931 and hit .316 with 2,880 hits and 1,244 runs batted in.

Frisch retired as a player in 1937. Ten years later, he was inducted into the Hall of Fame, becoming just the second Cardinal to accomplish that feat.

As for Ruth, by catching Frisch's fly out in foul territory in 1928, Ruth made up from what happened in 1926, when he was caught stealing second for the final out in game seven of Fall Classic against St. Louis.

But that didn't put a damper to his excellent 21-year career. One of the greatest home run hitters of all time, Ruth was among the first group to be selected to the Hall of Fame in 1936. Ruth was in first all-time in home runs with 714 before Hank Aaron broke it in 1974. He also hit .342 with 2,873 hits and 2,213 RBIs. Even though he's no longer No. 1 in home runs, he has the major league record in career slugging percentage at .690.

Wagner also was part of that first Hall of Fame class in 1936 that also included Ty Cobb, Walter Johnson and Christy Mathewson. Wagner, who played for the Pirates for 17 years, hit .327 with 3,415 hits and 1,732 RBIs and won nine batting championships. The only thing that put a sting in his career was making the final out of the first World Series in 1903.

Wagner struck out for the final out in game eight of the Fall Classic against the Boston Americans (now Red Sox).

He would get his first World Series ring in 1909, when he helped the Bucs beat the Tigers in eight games.

The Pirates won another title in 1925 by beating the Senators in seven games. Goslin struck out in game seven to end Washington's hopes of its second straight championship.

Goslin played a total of 11 seasons with the Senators. He also played with the St. Louis Browns and Detroit Tigers. Goslin finished his career with a .316 batting average, 248 home runs, 1,609 runs batted in and 2,735 hits. He won a batting title in 1928.

Goslin was elected to the Hall of the Fame by the Veterans' Committee in 1968.

Out of the 96 players who made the final out, one was a famous baseball analyst – Tim McCarver.

McCarver has called baseball for all four major networks – ABC, CBS, NBC and FOX. He called his first World Series for ABC in 1985 as a last-minute replacement for Howard Cosell. McCarver retired after the 2013 World Series.

Before he was an announcer, McCarver was a player, playing for the Cardinals, Phillies, Expos and Red Sox for 21 years. He played on two World Series championship teams in 1964 and 1967.

But McCarver didn't bring home his third World Series ring in 1968. The Tigers came back from a three-games-to-one deficit to beat St. Louis four games to three. In game seven, McCarver popped up to Bill Freehan in foul territory for the final out of the game and the Series. He never played in another World Series again.

No matter if you're the best broadcaster in the world, the best manager in baseball, the best hitter of baseball, best fielder in the baseball or the player who has the most friends on Facebook, every player dreads that final out of the World Series.

When players make the final out of the World Series, they'll have this grim look at their face, knowing that the baseball season is over. Walking back to the dugout and watching the other team celebrate a world championship is a painful feeling for players, even for pinch hitters.

In the 110-year history of the World Series, a total of 19 pinch hitters made the final out of the World Series, more than any other position. At one point, pinch hitters made the final out of the Fall Classic three years in a row from 1940-1942.

The last pinch hitter who made the final out was Tampa Bay's Eric Hinske in 2008. He came in to pinch hit for shortstop Jason Bartlett with a runner on second in the top of the ninth and the Rays were trailing the Phillies 4-3 in the fifth game at Citizens Bank Park. But Hinske couldn't drive in the tying run as Brad Lidge struck him out for the final out of the game, the Series and the 2008 season. It was Hinske's first and only season at Tampa Bay.

Boss Schmidt was the first pinch hitter to make the final out of the World Series. As a member of the Detroit Tigers, Schmidt flied out to Cubs shortstop Joe Tinker in game five for the last out of the 1907 World Series. The next year, Schmidt made the final out of the 1908 World Series. This time, he was the Tigers' catcher and this time, he grounded out to Cubs catcher Johnny Kling.

Schmidt is one of two hitters in World Series history who made the final out twice. The other one is Aaron Ward in 1921 and 1922, but the Yankees second baseman made up for that in game six of the 1923 World Series, fielding a ground ball hit by the New York Giants' Jack Bentley and throwing him out that clinched the Yankees' first of their 27 world titles.

Coincidentally, Bentley was a pinch hitter in the '23 Fall Classic. The other pinch hitters are Averill (1940), Bill Killefer (1915), Lew McCarty (1917), Jimmy Wasdell(1941), George Selkirk (1942), Mike Chartak (1944), Stan Lopata (1950), Sal Yvers (1951), Dale Mitchell (1954), Pat Corrales (1970), Von Joshua (1974), Lee Lacy (1977), Pat Kelly (1979), Mark Sweeney (1998), Orlando Palmeiro (2005) and Seth Smith (2007).

There were 14 second basemen and 13 left fielders who made the final out of the Series.

In 2013, Cardinals second baseman Matt Carpenter finished one hit shy from a 200-hit season. In game six of the World Series against Boston, Carpenter had three hits going into his at-bat against Koji Uehara, but he couldn't get the fourth hit as he struck out swinging.

Carpenter joined Davey Johnson (1969), Mark Lemke (1996), Larry Doyle (1913), Aaron Ward (1921 and 1922), Frankie Frisch (1928), Billy Herman (1938), Red Schoendienst (1958), Jerry Coleman (1957), Bobby Richardson (1964), Max Bishop (1931), Marty Barrett (1986), Tony Phillips (1988) and Carlos Baerga (1995) as the second basemen who were the final out of the Fall Classic.

"They outplayed us in this Series," Carpenter said. "It's a tough pill to swallow. We have a lot of be proud of with the year that we had. We have a bunch of guys who care about each other. It was a tough night for us. We hated to end it this way."

Texas' David Murphy was the last left fielder to make the final out of the World Series, flying out to St. Louis' Allen Craig in game seven of the 2011 Fall Classic at Busch

Stadium. The night before, Murphy thought he would be celebrating a world championship as the Rangers were one strike away – not once, but twice -- from winning it all. But Murphy and the Rangers' plans changed after Texas lost 10-9 in the sixth game and 6-2 in the seventh.

"This will never been a good feeling," Murphy told the St. Louis Post Dispatch on Oct. 30, 2011. "It hurts. It's hard to go through a full season and play so well and get to a Game 7 of a World Series and not get it done. There are so many positive things that we can take away from this year but right now it hurts. That's the easiest way to put it."

The other left fielders who were the last out are Pete Rose (1972), Goose Goslin (1925), Riggs Stephenson (1932), Debs Garms (1943), Willie McCovey (1962), Bob Allison (1965), Roy White (1976), Willie Wilson (1980), Elston Howard (1955), Les Mann (1918), Joe Jackson (1919) and Jo-Jo Moore (1937).

Nine third basemen made the final out of the World Series. Cabrera was the Tigers' third baseman when he struck out looking in game four in the 2012 Series. Ironically, the last third baseman who made the last out of the World Series was Brandon Inge, who also played for the Tigers.

Lave Cross (1905), Mike Mowrey (1916), Jackie Robinson (1956), Wayne Garrett (1973), Ron Cey (1978), Pinky Higgins (1946) and Carney Lansford (1990) were the other third basemen.

The last first baseman to make the final out was the Yankees' Bob Watson in 1981, when he flied out to Dodgers' center Ken Landreaux in game six at Yankee Stadium.

Six other first basemen made the last out of the Fall Classic –Yastremski (1975), Tom Jones (1909), Stuffy

McInnis (1914), Joe Kuhel (1933), Gil Hodges (1949) and George Scott (1967).

Wagner was the first player to make the last out of the World Series. He was the Pirates' shortstop in game eight of the 1903 Series. Five other shortstops made the final out, and they were Billy Rogell in 1934, Roy Hughes in 1945, Pee Wee Reese in 1952, Luis Aparicio in 1959 and Edgar Renteria in 2004.

Nine center fielders made the last out. Milwaukee's Gorman Thomas led the American League in home runs with 39 in the 1982 season. But with two outs in the top of the ninth in game seven of the '82 World Series against the Cardinals, Thomas didn't hit one out of the park. Sutter struck him out for the final out.

Ruth (1926), Nelson Cruz (2010), Andy Van Slyke (1985), Lou Johnson (1966), Tommy Holmes (1948), Hector Lopez (1963), Frank Schulte (1906) were the seven right fielders who made the final out.

Atlanta's Keith Lockhart was the first and only designated hitter to make the final out of the World Series when he flied out to Yankees' left fielder Chad Curtis in game four in 1999. It was Lockhart's only trip to the World Series.

THE LAST WORD

My mother, Rosie, never liked baseball or any other sport. She would always say, "Why would somebody run up and down the field and chasing a ball? That doesn't make any sense."

My mother was the first person who taught me whenever a team is losing – especially when it's your favorite team -- suck it up and be proud. In game seven of the 1985 World Series between the Cardinals and Royals, Kansas City stormed to a 2-0 lead after Darryl Motley hit a two-run homer in the bottom of the second. Then, I ran into my mother's room crying because the Cardinals were about to lose. She wasn't really sympathetic of me seeing my favorite team getting ready to lose a World Series after being up three games to one. She told me that I can't keep getting upset that the Cardinals are losing. She told me, 'They can't win all of the time!' So I sucked it up and went back to the living room and watched the rest of game seven, where the Cardinals lost their focus – and their minds -- and lost 11-0. If it weren't for my mom's talk, I wouldn't have gotten to see the final out. I saw Darryl Motley catch Andy Van Slyke's fly ball in right field and I had a little smile on my face. I was just happy to see a team win a World Series, even though it's not my favorite team. I was happy to see Motley make the final out.

(Speaking of Motley, I attempted three times on getting comments from the former Royal about getting the final out, but he turned down requests for an interview all three times).

I want to thank my mom for not only helping me suck it up, but writing this book. Even though she's not a sports fan, she raised me to work hard in whatever I do.

I want to thank my aunt Barbara Tate, who four years ago suggested that I should I write a book and I did.

I want to thank my sister Darlene, who allowed me to watch the final out of the 2012 World Series and helped me go back down memory lane, the time that she and I were pretending Bruce Sutter and Darrell Porter at our backyard.

I also want to thank Darin Erstad and Scott Brosius for giving up their busy time in helping me writing this book by giving their candid insight on what it means to get the final out of the World Series.

And I want to thank baseball. When the sport had that strike in 1994, my love of baseball had diminished. But as the Bible said, you have to forgive. I forgave baseball and I will continue to watch the World Series every year. Because baseball is good to the last out.

PLAYERS WHO GOT THE FINAL OUTS IN THE
WORLD SERIES
(BY TEAM)

Boston/Milwaukee/Atlanta Braves
1914 – Charlie Deal, third baseman
1957 – Eddie Mathews, third baseman
1995 – Marquis Grissom, center fielder

Baltimore Orioles
1966 – Paul Blair, left fielder
1970 – Brooks Robinson, third base
1983 – Cal Ripken, Jr., shortstop

Boston Red Sox
1903 – Bill Dinneen, pitcher
1915 – Everett Scott, shortstop
1916 – Everett Scott, shortstop
1918 – Dave Shean, second base
2004 – Keith Foulke, pitcher
2007 – Jonathan Papelbon, pitcher
2013 – Koji Uehara, pitcher

Chicago Cubs
1907 – Joe Tinker, shortstop
1908 – Johnny Kling, catcher

Chicago White Sox
1906 – Jiggs Donahue, first base
1917 – Eddie Collins, second base
2005 – Juan Uribe, shortstop

Cincinnati Reds
1919 – MorrieRath, second base
1940 – Lonny Frey, second base
1975 – Cesar Geronimo, center field
1976 – George Foster, left field
1990 – Todd Benzinger, first base

Cleveland Indians
1920 – Joe Sewell, second base
1948 – Bob Kennedy, left fielder

Detroit Tigers
1945 – Skeeter Webb, shortstop
1968 – Bill Freehan, catcher
1984 – Larry Herndon, left fielder

Kansas City Royals
1985 – Darryl Motley, right fielder

Los Angeles Angels/California Angels/Anaheim Angels/ Los Angeles Angels of Anaheim
2002 – Darin Erstad, center fielder

Brooklyn/Los Angeles Dodgers
1955 – Pee Wee Reese, shortstop
1959 – Wally Moon, left fielder
1963 – Maury Wills, shortstop
1965 – Sandy Koufax, pitcher
1981 – Ken Landreaux, center fielder
1988 – Orel Hershiser, pitcher

Florida/Miami Marlins
2003 – Josh Beckett, pitcher

Minnesota Twins
1987 – Gary Gaetti, third baseman

New York Mets
1969 – Cleon Jones, left fielder
1986 – Jesse Orosco, pitcher

New York Yankees
1923 – Aaron Ward, second base
1928 – Babe Ruth, left fielder
1932 – Ben Chapman, right fielder
1936 – Lou Gehrig, first baseman
1937 – Lou Gehrig, first baseman
1938 – Red Ruffing, pitcher
1939 – Frankie Crosetti, shortstop
1941 – Joe DiMaggio, center fielder
1943 – Joe Gordon, second base
1947 – SnuffyStirnweiss, second baseman
1949 – Joe Page, pitcher
1950 – Allie Reynolds, pitcher
1951 – Hank Bauer, right fielder
1952 – Gene Woodling, left fielder
1956 – Johnny Kucks, pitcher
1958 – Mickey Mantle, left fielder
1961 – Hector Lopez, left fielder
1962 – Bobby Richardson, second baseman
1977 – Mike Torrez, pitcher
1978 – Thurman Munson, catcher
1996 – Charlie Hayes, third baseman

1998 – Scott Brosius, third baseman
1999 – Chad Curtis, left fielder
2000 – Bernie Williams, center fielder
2009 – Robinson Cano, second baseman

Philadelphia/Oakland Athletics
1910 – Jack Barry, shortstop
1911 – Frank Baker, third base
1913 – Eddie Murphy, right fielder
1930 – Bing Miller, right fielder
1972 – Joe Rudi, left fielder
1973 – Bert Campaneris, shortstop
1974 – Rollie Fingers, pitcher
1989 – Tony Phillips, second baseman

Philadelphia Phillies
1980 – Tug McGraw, pitcher
2008 – Brad Lidge, pitcher

Pittsburgh Pirates
1909 – Fred Clarke, left fielder
1925 – Red Oldham, pitcher
1971 – Jackie Hernandez, shortstop
1979 – Omar Moreno, center fielder

St. Louis Cardinals
1926 – Bill O'Farrell, catcher
1931 – Pepper Martin, center fielder
1934 – Leo Durocher, shortstop
1942 – Jimmy Brown, second base
1944 – Ted Wilks, pitcher
1946 – Red Schoendienst, second base

1964 – Dal Maxvill, second base
1967 – Bob Gibson, pitcher
1982 – Bruce Sutter, pitcher
2006 – Adam Wainwright, pitcher
2011 – Allen Craig, left fielder

New York/San Francisco Giants
1905 – Bill Dahlen, shortstop
1921 – George Kelly, first baseman
1922 – Ross Youngs, right fielder
1933 – DolfLuque, pitcher
1954 – Hank Thompson, third base
2010 – Brian Wilson, pitcher
2012 – Sergio Romo, pitcher

Toronto Blue Jays
1992 – Mike Timlin, pitcher

PLAYERS WHO GOT THE FINAL OUTS IN THE WORLD SERIES (BY POSITION)

Pitcher (25)

1903 – Bill Dinneen, Boston Red Sox
1925 – Red Oldham, Pittsburgh Pirates
1933 – DolfLuque, New York Giants
1938 – Red Ruffing, New York Yankees
1944 – Ted Wilks, St. Louis Cardinals
1949 – Joe Page, New York Yankees
1950 – Allie Reynolds, New York Yankees
1956 – Johnny Kucks, New York Yankees
1965 – Sandy Koufax, Los Angeles Dodgers
1967 – Bob Gibson, St. Louis Cardinals
1974 – Rollie Fingers, Oakland A's
1977 – Mike Torrez, New York Yankees
1980 – Tug McGraw, Philadelphia Phillies
1982 – Bruce Sutter, St. Louis Cardinals
1986 – Jesse Orosco, New York Mets
1988 – Orel Hershiser, Los Angeles Dodgers
1992 – Mike Timlin, Toronto Blue Jays
2003 – Josh Burkett, Florida Marlins
2004 – Keith Foulke, Boston Red Sox
2006 – Adam Wainwright, St. Louis Cardinals
2007 – Jonathan Papelbon, Boston Red Sox
2008 – Brad Lidge, Philadelphia Phillies
2010 – Brian Wilson, San Francisco Giants
2012 – Sergio Romo, San Francisco Giants
2013 – Koji Uehara, Boston Red Sox

Catcher (4)
1908 – Johnny Kling, Chicago Cubs
1926 – Bob O'Farrell, St. Louis Cardinals
1968 – Bill Freehan, Detroit Tigers
1978 – Thurman Munson, New York Yankees

First base (4)
1906 – Jiggs Donahue, Chicago White Sox
1921 – George Kelly, New York Giants
1936 – Lou Gehrig, New York Yankees
1937 – Lou Gehrig, New York Yankees
1990 – Todd Benzinger, Cincinnati Reds

Second base (13)
1917 – Eddie Collins, Chicago White Sox
1918 – Dave Shean, Boston Red Sox
1919 – MorrieRath, Cincinnati Reds
1923 – Aaron Ward, New York Yankees
1940 – Lonny Frey, Cincinnati Reds
1942 – Jimmy Brown, St. Louis Cardinals
1943 – Joe Gordon, New York Yankees
1946 – Red Schoendienst, St. Louis Cardinals
1947 – Snuffy Stirnweiss, New York Yankees
1962 – Bobby Richardson, New York Yankees
1964 – Dal Maxvill, St. Louis Cardinals
1989 – Tony Phillips, Oakland A's
2009 – Robinson Cano, New York Yankees

Shortstop (14)
1905 – Bill Dahlen, New York Giants
1907 – Joe Tinker, Chicago Cubs
1910 – Jack Barry, Philadelphia A's

1915 – Everett Scott, Boston Red Sox
1916 – Everett Scott, Boston Red Sox
1920 – Joe Sewell, Cleveland Indians
1934 – Leo Durocher, St. Louis Cardinals
1939 – Frankie Crosetti, New York Yankees
1945 – Skeeter Webb, Detroit Tigers
1955 – Pee Wee Reese, Brooklyn Dodgers
1963 – Maury Wills, Los Angeles Dodgers
1971 – Jackie Hernandez, Pittsburgh Pirates
1973 – Bert Campancris, Oakland A's
1983 – Cal Ripken, Jr., Baltimore Orioles
2005 – Juan Uribe, Chicago White Sox

Third base (8)
1911 – Frank Baker, Philadelphia A's
1914 – Charlie Deal, Boston Braves
1954 – Hank Thompson, New York Giants
1957 – Eddie Mathews, Milwaukee Braves
1970 – Brooks Robinson, Baltimore Orioles
1987 – Gary Gaetti, Minnesota Twins
1996 – Charlie Hayes, New York Yankees
1998 – Scott Brosius, New York Yankees

Left field (12)
1909 – Fred Clarke, Pittsburgh Pirates
1928 – Babe Ruth, New York Yankees
1948 – Bob Kennedy, Cleveland Indians
1952 – Gene Woodling, New York Yankees
1959 – Wally Moon, Los Angeles Dodgers
1961 – Hector Lopez, New York Yankees
1969 – Cleon Jones, New York Mets
1972 – Joe Rudi, Oakland A's

1976 – George Foster, Cincinnati Reds
1984 – Larry Herndon, Detroit Tigers
1999 – Chad Curtis, New York Yankees
2011 – Allen Craig, St. Louis Cardinals

Center field (10)
1931 – Pepper Martin, St. Louis Cardinals
1941 – Joe DiMaggio, New York Yankees
1958 – Mickey Mantle, New York Yankees
1966 – Paul Blair, Baltimore Orioles
1975 – Cesar Geronimo, Cincinnati Reds
1979 – Omar Moreno, Pittsburgh Pirates
1981 – Ken Landreaux, Los Angeles Dodgers
1995 – Marquis Grissom, Atlanta Braves
2000 – Bernie Williams, New York Yankees
2002 – Darin Erstad, Anaheim Angels

Right field (6)
1913 – Eddie Murphy, Philadelphia A's
1922 – Ross Youngs, New York Giants
1930 – Bing Miller, Philadelphia A's
1932 – Ben Chapman, New York Yankees
1951 – Hank Bauer, New York Yankees
1985 – Darryl Motley, Kansas City Royals

PLAYERS WHO GOT THE FINAL
OUTS IN THE WORLD SERIES
(By Year)

(Note: The 1912, 1924, 1927, 1929, 1935, 1953, 1960, 1991, 1993, 1997 and 2001 World Series ended on a walk-off hit; the World Series wasn't played in 1904 and 1994)

1903 – Bill Dinneen, pitcher, Boston Red Sox
1905 – Bill Dahlen, shortstop, New York Giants
1906 – Jiggs Donahue, first baseman, Chicago White Sox
1907 – Joe Tinker, shortstop, Chicago Cubs
1908 – Johnny Kling, catcher, Chicago Cubs
1909 – Fred Clarke, left fielder, Pittsburgh Pirates
1910 – Jack Barry, shortstop, Philadelphia Athletics
1911 – Frank Baker, third base, Philadelphia Athletics
1913 – Eddie Murphy, right fielder, Philadelphia Athletics
1914 – Charlie Deal, third baseman, Boston Braves
1915 – Everett Scott, shortstop, Boston Red Sox
1916 – Everett Scott, shortstop, Boston Red Sox
1917 – Eddie Collins, second baseman, Chicago White Sox
1918 – Dave Shean, second baseman, Boston Red Sox
1919 – MorrieRath, second baseman, Cincinnati Reds
1920 – Joe Sewell, second baseman, Cleveland Indians
1921 – George "High Pockets" Kelly, first baseman, New York Giants
1922 – Ross Youngs, right fielder, New York Giants
1923 – Aaron Ward, second baseman, New York Yankees
1925 – Red Oldham, pitcher, Pittsburgh Pirates
1926 – Bob O'Farrell, catcher, St. Louis Cardinals
1928 – Babe Ruth, left fielder, New York Yankees
1930 – Bing Miller, right fielder, Philadelphia Athletics

1931 – Pepper Martin, center fielder, St. Louis Cardinals
1932 – Ben Chapman, right fielder, New York Yankees
1933 – Dolf Luque, pitcher, New York Giants
1934 – Leo Durocher, shortstop, St. Louis Cardinals
1936 – Lou Gehrig, first baseman, New York Yankees
1937 – Lou Gehrig, first baseman, New York Yankees
1938 – Red Ruffing, pitcher, New York Yankees
1939 – Frankie Crosetti, shortstop, New York Yankees
1940 – Lonny Frey, second baseman, Cincinnati Reds
1941 – Joe DiMaggio, center fielder, New York Yankees
1942 – Jimmy Brown, second baseman, St. Louis Cardinals
1943 – Joe Gordon, second baseman, New York Yankees
1944 – Ted Wilks, pitcher, St. Louis Cardinals
1945 – Skeeter Webb, shortstop, Detroit Tigers
1946 – Red Schoendienst, second baseman, St. Louis Cardinals
1947 – Snuffy Stirnweiss, second baseman, New York Yankees
1948 – Bob Kennedy, left fielder, Cleveland Indians
1949 – Joe Page, pitcher, New York Yankees
1950 – Allie Reynolds, pitcher, New York Yankees
1951 – Hank Bauer, right fielder, New York Yankees
1952 – Gene Woodling, left fielder, New York Yankees
1954 – Hank Thompson, third baseman, New York Giants
1955 – Pee Wee Reese, shortstop, Brooklyn Dodgers
1956 – Johnny Kucks, pitcher, New York Yankees
1957 – Eddie Mathews, third baseman, Milwaukee Braves
1958 – Mickey Mantle, center fielder, New York Yankees
1959 – Wally Moon, left fielder, Los Angeles Dodgers
1961 – Hector Lopez, left fielder, New York Yankees
1962 – Bobby Richardson, second baseman, New York Yankees
1963 – Maury Wills, shortstop, Los Angeles Dodgers
1964 – Dal Maxvill, second baseman, St. Louis Cardinals
1965 – Sandy Koufax, pitcher, Los Angeles Dodgers

1966 – Paul Blair, center fielder, Baltimore Orioles

1967 – Bob Gibson, pitcher, St. Louis Cardinals

1968 – Bill Freehan, catcher, Detroit Tigers

1969 – Cleon Jones, left fielder, New York Mets

1970 – Brooks Robinson, third baseman, Baltimore Orioles

1971 – Jackie Hernandez, shortstop, Pittsburgh Pirates

1972 – Joe Rudi, left fielder, Oakland A's

1973 – Bert Campaneris, shortstop, Oakland A's

1974 – Rollie Fingers, pitcher, Oakland A's

1975 – Cesar Geronimo, center fielder, Cincinnati Reds

1976 – George Foster, center fielder, Cincinnati Reds

1977 – Mike Torrez, pitcher, New York Yankees

1978 – Thurman Munson, catcher, New York Yankees

1979 – Omar Moreno, center fielder, Pittsburgh Pirates

1980 – Tug McGraw, pitcher, Philadelphia Phillies

1981 – Ken Landreaux, center fielder, Los Angeles Dodgers

1982 – Bruce Sutter, pitcher, St. Louis Cardinals

1983 – Cal Ripken, Jr., shortstop, Baltimore Orioles

1984 – Larry Herndon, left fielder, Detroit Tigers

1985 – Darryl Motley, right fielder, Kansas City Royals

1986 –Jesse Orosco, pitcher, New York Mets

1987 – Gary Gaetti, third baseman, Minnesota Twins

1988 – Orel Hershiser, pitcher, Los Angeles Dodgers

1989 – Tony Phillips, second baseman, Oakland A's

1990 – Todd Benzinger, first baseman, Cincinnati Reds

1992 – Mike Timlin, pitcher, Toronto Blue Jays

1995 – Marquis Grissom, center fielder, Atlanta Braves

1996 – Charlie Hayes, third baseman, New York Yankees

1998 – Scott Brosius, third baseman, New York Yankees

1999 – Chad Curtis, left fielder, New York Yankees

2000 – Bernie Williams, center fielder, New York Yankees

2002 – Darin Erstad, center fielder, Anaheim Angels

2003 – Josh Beckett, pitcher, Florida Marlins

2004 – Keith Foulke, pitcher, Boston Red Sox

2005 – Juan Uribe, shortstop, Chicago White Sox

2006 – Adam Wainwright, pitcher, St. Louis Cardinals

2007 – Jonathan Papelbon, pitcher, Boston Red Sox

2008 – Brad Lidge, pitcher, Philadelphia Phillies

2009 – Robinson Cano, second baseman, New York Yankees

2010 – Brian Wilson, pitcher, San Francisco Giants

2011 – Allen Craig, left fielder, St. Louis Cardinals

2012 – Sergio Romo, pitcher, San Francisco Giants

2013 – Koji Uehara, pitcher, Boston Red Sox

HITTERS WHO WERE THE FINAL OUTS IN THE WORLD SERIES
(By year)

1903 – Honus Wagner, shortstop, Pittsburgh Pirates (struck out)

1905 – Lave Cross, third baseman, Philadelphia Athletics (grounded out to shortstop)

1906 – Frank Schulte, right fielder, Chicago Cubs (grounded to first base)

1907 – Boss Schmidt, pinch hitter, Detroit Tigers (popped out to shortstop)

1908 – Boss Schmidt, catcher, Detroit Tigers (grounded out at home plate)

1909 – Tom Jones, first baseman, Detroit Tigers (popped out to left field)

1910 – Jimmy Archer, catcher, Chicago Cubs (tagged out by shortstop on force play)

1911 – Art Wilson, catcher, New York Giants (grounded out to third base)

1913 – Larry Doyle, second baseman, New York Giants (popped out to right field)

1914 – Stuffy McInnis, first baseman, Philadelphia A's (grounded out to third base)

1915 – Bill Killefer, pinch hitter, Philadelphia Phillies (grounded out to shortstop)

1916 – Mike Mowrey, third baseman, Brooklyn Robins (grounded out to shortstop)

1917 – Lew McCarty, pinch hitter, New York Giants (grounded out to second base)

1918 – Les Mann, left fielder, Chicago Cubs (grounded out to second base)

1919 – Joe Jackson, left fielder, Chicago White Sox (grounded out to second base)

1920 – Hy Myers, center fielder, Brooklyn Robins (forced out at second base)

1921 – Aaron Ward, second baseman, New York Yankees (was thrown out at third base)

1922 – Aaron Ward, second baseman, New York Yankees (popped out to right field)

1923 – Jack Bentley, pinch hitter, New York Giants (grounded out to second base

1925 – Goose Goslin, left fielder, Washington Senators (struck out)

1926 – Babe Ruth, right fielder, New York Yankees (caught stealing at second)

1928 – Frankie Frisch, second baseman, St. Louis Cardinals (popped out to left field)

1930 – Jimmie Wilson, catcher, St. Louis Cardinals (popped out to right field)

1931 – Max Bishop, second baseman, Philadelphia Athletics (popped out to center field)

1932 – Riggs Stephenson, left fielder, Chicago Cubs (popped out to right field)

1933 – Joe Kuhel, first baseman, Washington Senators (struck out)

1934 – Billy Rogell, shortstop, Detroit Tigers (forced out at second base by shortstop)

1936 – Harry Danning, catcher, New York Giants (grounded out to first base)

1937 – Jo-Jo Moore, left fielder, New York Giants (grounded out to first base)

1938 – Billy Herman, second baseman, Chicago Cubs (grounded out to pitcher)

1939 – Wally Berger, center fielder, Cincinnati Reds (lined out to shortstop)

1940 – Earl Averill, pinch hitter, Detroit Tigers (grounded out to second base)

1941 – Jimmy Wasdell, pinch hitter, Brooklyn Dodgers (popped out to center field)

1942 – George Selkirk, pinch hitter, New York Yankees (grounded out to second base)

1943 – Debs Garms, left fielder, St. Louis Cardinals (grounded out to second base)

1944 – Mike Chartak, pinch hitter, St. Louis Browns (struck out)

1945 – Roy Hughes, shortstop, Chicago Cubs (forced out at second by shortstop)

1946 – Pinky Higgins, third baseman, Boston Red Sox (forced out at second by second baseman)

1947 – Bruce Edwards, catcher, Brooklyn Dodgers (grounded into double play)

1948 – Tommy Holmes, right fielder, Boston Braves (popped out to left field)

1949 –Gil Hodges, first baseman, Brooklyn Dodgers (struck out)

1950 – Stan Lopata, pinch hitter, Philadelphia Phillies (struck out)

1951 – Sal Yvers, pinch hitter, New York Giants (lined out to right field)

1952 – Pee Wee Reese, shortstop, Brooklyn Dodgers (popped out to left field)

1954 – Dale Mitchell, pinch hitter, Cleveland Indians (popped out to third base)

1955 – Elston Howard, left fielder, New York Yankees (grounded out to shortstop)

1956 – Jackie Robinson, third baseman, Brooklyn Dodgers (struck out)

1957 – Jerry Coleman, second baseman, New York Yankees (forced out at third base)

1958 – Red Schoendienst, second baseman, Milwaukee Braves (popped out to center field)

1959 – Luis Aparicio, shortstop, Chicago White Sox (popped out to left field)

1961 – Vada Pinson, center fielder, Cincinnati Reds (popped out to left field)

1962 – Willie McCovey, left fielder, San Francisco Giants (lined out to second base)

1963 – Hector Lopez, right fielder, New York Yankees (grounded out to shortstop)

1964 – Bobby Richardson, second baseman, New York Yankees (popped out to second)

1965 – Bob Allison, left fielder, Minnesota Twins (struck out)

1966 – Lou Johnson, right fielder, Los Angeles Dodgers (popped out to center field)

1967 – George Scott, first baseman, Boston Red Sox (struck out)

1968 – Tim McCarver, catcher, St. Louis Cardinals (popped foul to catcher)

1969 – Cleon Jones, left fielder, New York Mets (popped out to left field)

1970 – Pat Corrales, pinch hitter, Cincinnati Reds (grounded out to third base)

1971 – MervRettenmund, center fielder, Baltimore Orioles (grounded to shortstop)

1972 – Pete Rose, left fielder, Cincinnati Reds (popped out to left field)

1973 – Wayne Garrett, third baseman, New York Mets (popped out to shortstop)

1974 – Von Joshua, pinch hitter, Los Angeles Dodgers (grounded out to pitcher)

1975 – Carl Yastremski, first baseman, Boston Red Sox (popped out to center field)

1976 – Roy White, left fielder, New York Yankees (popped out to left field)

1977 – Lee Lacy, pinch hitter, Los Angeles Dodgers (popped out to pitcher)

1978 – Ron Cey, third baseman, Los Angeles Dodgers (popped foul to catcher)

1979 – Pat Kelly, left fielder, Baltimore Orioles (popped out to center field)

1980 – Willie Wilson, left fielder, Kansas City Royals (struck out)

1981 – Bob Watson, first baseman, New York Yankees (popped out to center field)

1982 – Gorman Thomas, center fielder, Milwaukee Brewers (struck out)

1983 – Garry Maddox, center fielder, Philadelphia Phillies (lined out to shortstop)

1984 – Tony Gwynn, right fielder, San Diego Padres (popped out to left field)

1985 – Andy Van Slyke, right fielder, St. Louis Cardinals (popped out to right field)

1986 – Marty Barrett, second baseman, Boston Red Sox (struck out)

1987 – Willie McGee, center fielder, St. Louis Cardinals (grounded out to third base)

1988 – Tony Phillips, second baseman, Oakland A's (struck out)

1989 – Brett Butler, center fielder, San Francisco Giants (grounded out to second base)

1990 – Carney Lansford, third baseman, Oakland A's (popped out to first base)

1992 – Otis Nixon, center fielder, Atlanta Braves (grounded out to pitcher)

1995 – Carlos Baerga, second baseman, Cleveland Indians (popped out to center field)

1996 – Mark Lemke, second baseman, Atlanta Braves (popped out to third base)

1998 – Mark Sweeney, pinch hitter, San Diego Padres (grounded out to third base)

1999 – Keith Lockhart, designated hitter, Atlanta Braves (popped out to left field)

2000 – Mike Piazza, catcher, New York Mets (popped out to center field)

2002 – Kenny Lofton, center fielder, San Francisco Giants (popped out to center field)

2003 – Jorge Posada, catcher, New York Yankees (tagged out by pitcher)

2004 – Edgar Renteria, shortstop, St. Louis Cardinals (grounded out to pitcher)

2005 – Orlando Palmeiro, pinch hitter, Houston Astros (grounded out to shortstop)

2006 – Brandon Inge, third baseman, Detroit Tigers (struck out)

2007 – Seth Smith, pinch hitter, Colorado Rockies (struck out)

2008 – Eric Hinske, pinch hitter, Tampa Bay Rays (struck out)

2009 – Shane Victorino, center fielder, Philadelphia Phillies (grounded out to second base)

2010 – Nelson Cruz, right fielder, Texas Rangers (struck out)

2011 – David Murphy, left fielder, Texas Rangers (popped out to left field)

2012 – Miguel Cabrera, third baseman, Detroit Tigers (struck out)

2013 – Matt Carpenter, second baseman, St. Louis Cardinals (struck out)